a year of loving kindness to myself

& OTHER ESSAYS

a year of loving kindness to myself

& OTHER ESSAYS

BRIGID LOWRY

This book is dedicated to
my dear friends and lovely family.

CONTENTS

Prajna 7
A year of loving kindness to myself 9
- January: Beginning 9
- February: Slowing down 11
- March: Having fun 15
- April: Working with difficulty 20
- May: Loving kindness to my feelings 23
- June: Equanimity 28
- July: Acceptance 32
- August: Anxiety 35
- September: On wonder 40
- October: Solitude and connection 45
- November: Living simply 50
- December: Creativity 55

On New Year's Eve, a prayer 58
Unable to save the many beings 60
On journals, notebooks, diaries and me 62
On Friday 67
On death 71
On things to do when life goes sideways 74
On friendship 75

Onwards 78
On solace 80
On walking 84
A few of my dreams 87
On Singapore 88
On house-sitting 91
On the spiritual life 94
On an ordinary day 100
For Tony Hoagland 106
On thinking 108
Border lines 113
Life lessons 114
On gratitude and joy 117
On questions 120
On decision-making 122
On the singing heart kitchen 126
On travel 129
Following the moon home 133
On sitting quietly 134
Things not written about 138
Notes and acknowledgements 140

PRAJNA

All your pretty dresses won't save you.
You can't wriggle out of it.
The suffering of this floating world
will continue to present itself.
Just keep on being the Buddha,
white flowers in your open arms.

A YEAR OF LOVING KINDNESS TO MYSELF

JANUARY: BEGINNING

I commit to treating myself with tender acceptance.

I dedicate the coming year to the practice of loving kindness to myself. Why?

Because my childhood was pretty shit.

Because I can't be kind to anyone else until I learn how to be kind to myself.

Because I do not know how to be kind to myself. No-one taught me. As a child, my parents did not model loving kindness. They were too busy drinking.

Because I'm unhappy and I've gleaned enough insight to see that much of my unhappiness is self-created.

Because, as Anne Lamott says, life is amazing, but also weird and hard.

Because the Dalai Lama says kindness is his religion and I want to feel like his smile, at least some of the time.

Sometimes she is very loud. The witchy voice, the one who says: They didn't text you back because they don't like you. Your hair looks awful. You shouldn't have said that. Your appetites are dangerous. Nothing you do will ever be good enough. Do not be the way you are.

Thinking this way leads down a dark bleak road to nowhere good. I am so tired of being a prisoner in a self-created cage of Me-Not-Okay.

It's summer, a time of swimming, ice-cream, music, the languid pleasures of the season.

What will this year bring? Can I learn a new way to be?

FEBRUARY: SLOWING DOWN

There is plenty of time.

Summer holidays are over. People are returning from wherever they've been. School begins. It's very hot. Rude drivers, cranky kids, hassled parents.

I'm miserable about the ending of my relationship. My mind keeps chewing away at the past, processing who did what, trying to make sense of it, but it can't be solved this way. It was what it was. Now it is over. I notice myself trying to fill the emptiness with plans and activities.

It's an old pattern for me, hurrying into the future. Slowing down and fully inhabiting this moment is a lifetime challenge.

'You're up and down like a botfly,' my father-in-law would tease.

'You've always got a list and you never stay long,' a friend accused.

I am not alone in this behaviour. It's common, because

the imaginary Better Next Bit is such a seductive fantasy, especially when the present moment is confronting.

Why is it so hard to just stop and relax? Sally Kempton suggests that the ego's addiction to busyness has, at its core, a terror of its own emptiness.

Always being busy can become relentless, meaningless. No time to know anything fully, no time to savour the immediate. Our culture has led us to believe that doing and achieving more is better—but rising rates of stress, anxiety, depression, heart disease and cancer are not a good sign. It's important to take responsibility for our own mental health and wellbeing, not just for ourselves but for those who love us, and for the society we live in.

Not just for me, but for my grandchildren and my community, I commit to living in a healthy way, gently, creatively and with merriment.

I am practising doing one less thing, rather than one more thing. I'm trying to do each thing fully instead of juggling three things at once. I am learning to love and respect my body and not push on regardless.

Practising like this helps me stay connected with the simplicity and richness of the moment. Slowing down to the speed of now sounds easy but it takes effort, actually. It's not so hard when it is a beautiful here and now and we're feeling good, though even then we may miss the true taste of the moment if we're not in touch with it long enough to savour it. As for being present with the more difficult emotions, it may seem counterintuitive but it is a wise thing to do. Being true to our humanity, to our shabby corners and dark places, can be deeply healing. Human weather comes and goes, no problem, when we relax enough to let it.

Zen teacher Ross Bolleter teaches a helpful practice called The Five Ring Circus of Now, which is good to do anytime, with a spirit of adventure.

Begin by taking an upright posture, relaxing into the body. Start to notice the breath, simple and easy. When you feel steady with that, include sounds. If you get lost, return to the breath. Expand the attention to include breath, sound, and sensation in the body: the itchy knee, tension in the belly, whatever is rolling. When you get lost, return to the breath. Widen the attention to include how you are feeling: tired, sad, calm, whatever mood is present for you. Getting lost, return to the breath. Finally, include thoughts. Notice thoughts arise but leave them alone, gently letting them come and go. This is a wonderful method for resting easy in the moment, right where you are.

◇◇◇◇◇◇◇◇

Sunday. I leave it until the last minute to go somewhere I'd planned to go. When the time arrives, I'm exhausted. It's hard to abandon the idea of going and surrender to the reality of being too tired.

I make a cup of tea instead, and sit to enjoy it. Or that's the plan. Instead I hear the voice. The crippling one that blames, shames, negates and catastrophises.

You should have gone. Why didn't you go earlier in the week? You don't measure up. You can't get things together. You're not coping.

I refuse to accept this analysis of the situation. What a squandering, to spend the evening torturing myself about resting up. It's new to me to really listen to my energy level and act accordingly. I can't do everything. I don't have to explain myself to anybody, or justify my decision. It is my right to say no to something, and not guilt myself about it.

What is loving kindness to myself, really? It is stopping before I get exhausted, buying myself a favourite food when I'm feeling low, listening to things that nourish and inspire me, yoga for a sore back, a book beside the bed.

This is it, right now, the good bit, the only bit, I tell myself. Just do your best, one foot in front of the other, and take your time.

MARCH: HAVING FUN

Treating myself like a precious object will make me strong.

I did not learn fun in my early life. I lived in a big sad old house with my two messy alcoholic parents, and I learned to keep quiet, to survive, to get by. I see myself in photographs. A solemn child. School was no fun, either, although intellectually interesting at times. As a young woman, a life of sex, drugs and rock'n'roll was fun for a while, but proved futile as a true road to serenity. As an adult I learned to achieve things, live sensibly, return library books on time, write books, save money, make food go a long way, be a dutiful citizen. Having fun, however, has not been my specialty area.

When I was little, books were my fun. However shit my day was, however violent the atmosphere, I could escape into the pages, and hang out with imaginary people whose lives were excellent. I liked *Bunchy* by Joyce Lankester

Brisley, about a girl having fun and creative imaginings in her gentle grandmother's house. I read and re-read *Drovers Road* by Joyce West, set in New Zealand's rugged South Island, in which Merry, Gay, Hugh and Eve had splendid adventures on their horses. I loved *The Good Master* by Kate Seredy, about a madcap girl in big petticoats, her kind aunt and uncle, wild horses and a boy cousin who didn't like the girl at first but later became a dear companion.

Eloise by Kay Thompson was another of my favourite books. It's the wonderfully illustrated story of a girl living in a hotel in New York with her nanny. She skibbles around the hotel, having maximum fun and creating innocent mayhem. She orders room service: a raisin for her turtle and a beef bone for her little pugdog, watches TV with her nanny, annoys the staff and other residents, and generally has a fine old time. My granddaughter also loves this book, and we have read it often.

◇◇◇◇◇◇◇◇

Having dedicated this month to having fun, I decide that my granddaughter and I shall have a joyous experience together, as a birthday treat for me. I book us a night in a hotel by the beach, which has sea views and room service. We discuss room service.

'Will there be spring rolls?' my granddaughter asks. She

made spring rolls at school recently, using vegies picked from the kitchen garden.

'Not sure. Maybe.'

'How about light chocolate?'

She is keen to know about this, as her parents eat bitter chocolate. She's not allowed much sugar, but is fond of the occasional chocolate bear or light chocolate of any kind.

'Possibly. I think it's mainly things like a chicken toasted sandwich, with chips.'

'Okay.' She nods agreeably. 'Can I order?'

'Yes, you can.'

◇◇◇◇◇◇◇◇

We like our room and the view of the sea from our balcony. We like walking out the doors to the park, the skate park and the ocean. We sit up in bed at six am, watching cartoons, her with a tiny pot of ice-cream, me with a stiff cup of tea. We order room service for dinner and eat breakfast in a café beside the sea. When we cash our free drink voucher in the restaurant, she meets a chocolate thickshake for the first time in her life.

'God, this is the loveliest thing I have ever tasted,' she says, and keeps on drawing mermaids.

When we play at the pool she tells me that mermaids should wave their arms when they swim. I mishear, and think she is saying that mermaids should wave their arses when they swim. Either way, they totally should. On the way home we agree that this would be an annual event.

Splurging out on a special occasion without worrying about the expense is something I've rarely done. It is delicious.

◇◇◇◇◇◇◇◇

Fun is individual. It can be practised by oneself, or in company. It doesn't have to be elaborate, or cost money.

My fun vibe now includes stepping on crunchy food when I see it on the pavement, silly walks, weird face competitions, ice-cream, playing in the ocean, hanging out with happy people, dancing around the living room, dressing up.

What's your idea of fun? Fun is not an idea, it's an activity, and an outlook. Let's live merrily. Let's make like the Dalai Lama. His religion is kindness and his stated aim is to be happy.

◇◇◇◇◇◇◇◇

March 25.

May the next bit be the best bit, I write on other people's birthday cards. Today I am nearer to death than I have ever been but this is it, now or never, my chance to be fully alive.

I buy sourdough, mangoes, nectarines, a black cushion with red flowers, a soft blue rug. Happy Birthday to me. *May the next bit be the best bit.*

APRIL: WORKING WITH DIFFICULTY

I vow to open my arms to all of it.

April is my saddest month. I don't know why, but it always has been. Something about the end of summer, the melancholy of the darkening days. I can't fully explain it, but there it is.

As always, I sit in morning meditation. My experience is not necessarily one of joyous white light, ease and bliss. Far from. Today my mind is restless and my body is a shifting landscape of unpleasant sensations.

I take some deep breaths and relax, then sweep my attention from head to toe, noticing tension, loosening into the sensations as much as I can, softening body and mind. Over and over again, I let out my breath, letting it flow easy. Rather than trying to make anything go away, I just sit, noticing. When I include it, the dread in my belly melts into raggedy sadness containing not only my own sorrows but the endless sorrows of the world. When I can allow things to be as they actually are, my sitting is more tender, more peaceful. This is just the way things are, for now. Might as well surrender, bow down without complaint.

Tara Brach calls this approach radical acceptance. It really is radical. To resist nothing. To greet whatever arises with *Thank you, I accept.*

Regarding difficulty as an honoured guest is not our common response. However, difficulty can be a place of learning, although the lessons are not always easy ones.

What is to be seen here? How much of this misery is created by my own thinking? What could I let go of? Is there anything practical I can do to sort my current problems or is it wiser to allow things to take their course, trusting that this will sort out by itself?

It can feel counterintuitive to lavish ourselves with care and love when we are mired in self-loathing or despair because, let's face it, you don't deserve anything good, or that is what your evil-twin self will tell you. I have learned that the worse I feel, the more I need to cultivate self-care and self-compassion. This is not a fixed position. It's a daily dance, listening deeply to body and heart, trusting that life is taking me where it is most beneficial to go.

When I am low, it is harder to notice good moments but even the shittiest day contains small mercies and tiny blessings:

Finding a clean old-fashioned wooden peg in the rubbish, perfect for making a peg doll with a poppy petal skirt, pipe cleaner arms and a tiny drawn-on face.

My happy-place café: the barista with his droll sense of humour, two friendly waitresses, a pot of prana chai, milky and not too sweet.

Exchanging a smile with the woman sitting on the pavement rolling a cigarette while her boyfriend opens a cask of cheap white wine. She has the most amazing grin.

The little ordinary pleasures of this life, bringing comfort on a difficult day.

Kindness is a cup of tea and painkillers when you need them. Kindness is letting yourself be sad when sadness comes, making room for tenderness to your own pain. It's permission to get things wrong, to be silly, to admit that something is too much for you. It's knowing that you can't solve anyone's problems but that a listening ear, a quiet heart and cake might be of use. It's remembering that this too will pass, which is a truth harder to love in the good times, but quite useful in the difficult ones.

MAY: LOVING KINDNESS TO MY FEELINGS

It's already here. Let me feel it.

During my time living in a Buddhist monastery, the resident monk gave the community members dharma names. The name given to me was Metta, meaning 'Loving Kindness'. I thought this was because I was shining with radiant love, but it wasn't.

'You have a lot of anger,' the monk informed me. Metta was the name I was being asked to grow into. The name he had been given by his teacher was Khantipalo, Teacher of Patience, because he was impatient.

Fair enough. I didn't want to admit it, but it was true. I can do nice, I can do kind, but when I get angry, a wild Irish woman appears, ablaze with fury. I find her terrifying.

Similarly, I find it hard to come to terms with my fear, my shame, my judgmental mind, my envy, my loneliness, my anxiety. These are all normal feelings for a human being but many people spend a lifetime repressing and denying challenging feelings, or trying to replace them with more pleasant ones. For meditators and yoga practitioners, the latter is known as spiritual bypassing, or more colloquially, sugar on shit. Falsely claiming peace, love and happiness is a losing game, as Jung so kindly pointed out. When shadow is unacknowledged, it runs the show in underhand and devious ways.

The saddest, strangest, shabbiest parts of me, despised and ignored for so long, need my tenderness the most. Avoiding them denies what is real. I want to live authentically. Inner struggle is painful and fruitless, and only compounds the difficulty.

'You are all already perfect and you can all use a little improvement,' Suzuki Roshi told his students. How lovely to start with the idea that there's basically nothing wrong with me. I'm not broken and I don't need fixing. Zen is full of paradox, so if I am already perfect, what needs improvement then? I'd say it's the ability to be real with my stuff, instead of trying to pretend it away. What I'm aiming for is a heart and mind big enough to hold it all, every goddamn bit: the hurt, the yearning, the overwhelm, the self-doubt and midnight fears.

Feelings are challenging, but it's never as bad as you think. As Jeff Foster writes, 'The worst thing you'll ever have to face in this life is a thought, a sensation, a feeling, a sound, a smell, happening in this moment.'

Firstly, simply name what's going on: Fear. Hurt. Grief. Shame. It is clear and honest to identify what is happening, to give it a place. Keep it real. If you are angry, be angry. If you are sad, be sad. Avoid minimising and repressing.

The next step is to allow the feeling in the body as pure sensation. Breathing into the body, softly, with kindness. Tight belly, heaviness around the eyes, clenched jaw. That's all.

Things pass a lot quicker once we allow them in. It's pointless to rationalise the feeling, try to make sense of it or hurry it away, figure out who to blame, or tell the story over and over again until you come out on top. Endless ruminating only magnifies the situation, and adheres it to you further.

Our emotions feel like our own gig but they don't belong to us, not really. They are manifestations of human weather, nothing more, nothing less. Widening the sky and seeing my emotions as human, not exclusively my own, helps me to loosen their grip. By recognising my stuff and gently feeling it in my body until it shifts and eases, life becomes a whole lot easier. More spacious. At the very least, I don't make things any worse, because acting in an angry or mean-spirited way can lead to a shitload of trouble.

It's a holy task, to trust myself, resting easy with what I'm feeling, relaxing around the edges. Holding whatever arises delicately, accepting that this is just the way it is, for now.

An example. While writing this book, I hit an Oh-Shit moment. I'd collected pages of fragments, half-written thoughts and possible ideas but I was having trouble working out what went where. Energy and enthusiasm, low. Faith in my own ability, marginal. I decide to rename a document but instead, oh no, please no, I have deleted the entire document.

I have no idea how to recover lost files. Disbelief. Panic. Anger.

My computer skills are limited. Despite feverish Google research I can't work out how to retrieve it. I'm distraught, disheartened and late for my volunteering gig at the op shop where I help with the books. As soon as I arrive, a woman I find tricky informs me I've culled too many books. Furthermore, her way of shelving books is superior to mine, apparently.

I excuse myself, go into the garden and shed a few tears. I am overwhelmed, angry with myself about my technological ineptitude, pissed off with the picky woman. It all sucks and I don't like any of it. The irony being, of course, that I'm writing about feelings being okay.

Once again I notice my old patterns of recrimination,

melodrama and agitation, but I don't buy into them. I sit quietly, looking at the nasturtium leaves, feeling the sensations in my body, the self-pity, the anger, the shame. I tell the woman I'll see her another day when I'm feeling more cheerful. She's relieved, I imagine, that I don't embark on a massive debriefing or bombard her with argument. Not worth making a big deal about this. I take myself home. Eat a mandarin. Sort out the computer thing. Feel okay again. As the Dalai Lama once said: after forty years of practice, I think I can see a little progress.

JUNE: EQUANIMITY

May I be at ease in the flow of life.

Bare trees. Warmer clothes. More bedding. Winter always comes as a revelation here in Perth. Summer feels endless. Golden days, beach, days of frolic and play. Autumn is a short season, barely noticeable and then, suddenly, what a surprise, the days shorten and everything changes for the cooler.

Like the seasons, life is fluid. Everything is in a state of flux, all the time, including us. Sometimes we don't notice this. The days roll into each other, routines are followed, everything feels same old same old, but the changing seasons remind us that trees, flowers and temperatures are never static and neither are people or events. It's vastly shocking when something major happens, either to yourself, a loved one, or in the wider world, and we realise how little agency we have over life and what it delivers.

There is actually a great liberation when we fully

acknowledge that we have no idea what comes next, but there is also vulnerability. It can be terrifying, especially for those who have suffered traumatic life events.

Equanimity has never been my strong suit. As far back as I can remember, I was labelled oversensitive. I wonder if I was born that way, or whether it was a result of living with alcoholism, neglect, violence, suicide. Whatever the cause, I have never been the steadiest peanut in the pack. I am easily tumbled around by the vicissitudes of living, so the cultivation of a calm and steady mind is imperative for me.

Suffering has been defined as the mind unable to accommodate its experience. However, it isn't usually the experience that is the problem, it's our relationship to it. When I add anxiety and fear to my moments—worrying about something that has already happened or catastrophising about what might happen—I add a double whammy of suffering. If I stick with what is actually happening, the moment is bearable. When I accept the real, without avoidance, I discover a bedrock of ease and grace. As Zen teacher Glenn Wallis reminds his students, 'Stay current.' It takes effort to do this because old patterns are deeply ingrained. It means being mindful of what is happening right now, accepting it, and abandoning unhelpful thinking, over and over, from now until forever. I have found that if I stay in my body, focusing on something obvious like the sensation of my feet on the ground, even when bad news strikes, the moment feels bearable.

Lately, when I get home for the day, I have a hot shower and put on my creative loungewear, aka pyjamas. Then I lie down on my bed, relaxing my body and silently reciting equanimity phrases:

May I stand steady in the face of difficulty. May I be at ease in the flow of life.

Finding phrases that feel right, and varying them when they feel stale, keeps the practice alive.

This is just the way things are, for now. Peacefully I meet the changing moment.

I really look forward to this daily practice now. It's a treat. Relaxing like this brings composure and enhances my ability to live with good cheer. I still have to deal with the end of my partnership, the challenges of aging and the horrors of world politics, but I am able to do so with more equanimity.

Equanimity isn't coldness. It is not indifference. It includes whatever is occurring, and takes an interest in it. Equanimity is grace in the face of difficulty. It means not requiring things to be otherwise. It is a state of mind to be cultivated, in order to deal more wisely with whatever arises.

May I be a wise old tree, standing steady, in the midst of my sorrow, my fear, my heartache. May I be, as Zen practice suggests, a lotus at home in the muddy water.

JULY: ACCEPTANCE

Perfect, just as it is.

It's cold. I don't like it. I've never been fond of winter. Childhood memories of grey days, chilblains, ancient hot water bottles, drab coats.

Life feels tough, actually. I'm still mourning the loss of my partnership. It's very painful and also awkward, as we live in the same apartment block.

I wanted it to work out. Or if it didn't work out, at least to have a civilised ending. As yet, not so. Sometimes, by mistake, I find myself yearning for him, even though I was the one who left, even though we were a hopeless match. I'm like an alcoholic craving a drink, despite knowing it would be ruinous.

How much difficulty I cause myself when I am at odds with circumstance. Krishnamurti famously said that his secret was that he didn't mind what happened. Man, he was onto something. I'm trying to reconcile myself with the way things actually are, which is not as one might have liked. I do know, really, that if I can love what life brings me, I'll be happy. More or less.

Suzuki Roshi, leading a retreat, began a sentence with 'The problems you are experiencing now …' The yogis waited for him to tell them that their problems would go away due to their excellent meditation, but he concluded with '… will continue for the rest of your life.' It's true. However many problems we have, our biggest problem is that we don't want to have any problems.

'Let's do winter. Let me feel the season,' my friend writes. She is a Jungian, and wise. It's encouraging.

Winter has its own beauty. The glassy stillness of the lake, the crisp air, the fading pale blue light, the warmth of home to come home to. It's a time of hibernation, of hot beverages, warm coats, fabulous scarves and cosy beanies, a time of dressing-gowns, slippers, books, soup. It's double rainbows and bright umbrellas. It's learning to come to terms with my life as it is, plain and simple, despite the fact that I'm messy with heartbreak, confused, lonely and sad. Still, I'm glad to be alive. I know I will get through this if I can surrender to it.

Acceptance is the practice of Yes. It's the ability to include everything, to love your fate, as Nietzsche said. Acceptance also involves resilience, which has been defined as a resolute acceptance of reality, a sense that life is meaningful and an exceptional ability to improvise. It involves embracing impermanence, because if everything is only temporary, there's no point making such a fuss about it.

The eight worldly winds—pleasure and pain, praise and blame, gain and loss, fame and disrepute—will blow forever. No escape. That's why meditation is useful. Sitting quietly allows us to be who we are, right where we are. We learn to be okay with whatever comes our way, with patience, with love. We learn to accept the present moment, just as it is.

So I sit every day. My teacher is this moment, this heartache, this winter sunshine.

◇◇◇◇◇◇◇◇

I just got my first-ever speeding ticket, for travelling sixty-three kilometres in a fifty-kilometre zone. Farewell, two hundred bucks. At least I have the money to pay it, and in a few weeks I'll have forgotten all about it. This proves I am getting better at acceptance. Meanwhile my mantra is: *Oh fuck. Oh well.*

AUGUST: ANXIETY

I am enough, I have enough.

Still cold, but sunny. Spring is surely just around a corner or two. At the lake, elegant striped ducks with six fluffy ducklings. In nearby gardens, jonquils, jasmine, the first pink blossoms on fruit trees. How can I be unhappy, with all this beauty around me? Well, when my mind is troubled, I can.

I have always lived with anxiety, sometimes at a low level, sometimes crippling. To have compassion for my own suffering in this regard, to learn how to live with it and not be so ruled by it, is a deep journey for me.

Anxiety comes from a groundswell of fear. It's waking up with heavy, nameless dread. It's fearing terrible things are about to happen. It's a tight jaw, negative self-talk and eyes that don't see the good stuff. Anxiety is an evil companion, always offering the worst-case scenario, and worrying is praying for the wrong things, as a wise monk observed.

The last few days have been tough. Anxiety abundant.

Usually I like looking after my son's house and dog while he and his family go away, but this time it has been a challenge. To begin with, I couldn't get a grip when packing for my week's sojourn. Travelling lightly is a foreign country for me. So many major decisions: how many pairs of slippers, which teas, how many books? I want to take all the food from my fridge, various art supplies, half my medicine cupboard, all my shoes and a partridge in a pear tree.

So I load my little car with too much stuff, and set forth, anxiety accompanying me. I like their house, in summer. It's big and airy and right next to a park. However, it has tiled floors and in winter, it's bloody cold. My son has given strict instructions that the little dog must not sleep in my bed. The little dog is not in accord. He scratches on the door all night, calling out in his sad doggie way. My bedroom is icy. I lie awake, fairly far from happy.

The next day, having given it much thought, I tell a friend that I won't be seeing her for a while. I've accompanied her through a long, tough patch but I need a break. I'm not enjoying being with her right now, and it's affecting my own mental health. She is dear to me, so this is hard to do. My friend takes it sorrowfully. We hold hands and agree to meet in a few months. Driving home, I am marginally relieved but also guilty, troubled, low.

A nice long walk at the beach will lift my spirits, I decide. I park the car, then realise that I badly need to pee. The toilet is miles away but there's nobody in sight, so I squat down behind a bush. As some of you may know, a lady bush-wee is not always successful and can result in pissing on one's own shoe, leg or skirt. In this case, trousers. Standing up, an abundance of brown muck squiggles up between my naked toes because I have trodden in a huge dog shit.

It seems that God does not want me to feel happy, easeful and relaxed right now. Instead I'm going to have to deal with feeling anxious, weird and wobbly, no matter how badly I wish to avoid it. So I walk on the beach, glad of the sand and the sea which washes away the crap on my foot, and vaguely eases the crap in my heart.

To greet difficulty as an honoured guest sounds easy, but mainly we do not do this. We greet difficulty as a totally unwanted visitor, and instantly have turned one hurdle into two, the original problem compounded by the stress and impossibility of trying to get rid of it.

This is all very well for *you* to say, you may argue, but I have real problems. My mother has Alzheimer's. My dog got run over. I have had a cancer diagnosis—fill in the blank.

Here's the thing, baby. We all have troubles. No-one, repeat no-one, is exempt. There's great hubris in thinking that we should have a life of no problems, because we're all in the same boat. Anxiety, fear, confusion, grief, loneliness, ambivalence, world-weariness, suffering of mind and body in every shape and form are unavoidably part of the human condition. They are our birthright, along with joy, delight, anticipation, and the tastier emotions.

I have heard this truth a thousand times. Yet here it is again, waiting for me to remember and understand it. *C'est la vie, n'est-ce pas?* My troubles are in the human realm and are absolutely minor compared to those of millions of other people.

Ezra Bayda writes about this in his excellent book *Aging for Beginners*. He is a Zen teacher who has faced extreme health problems and chronic pain, now living in an aged-care facility with his wife. He offers specific meditations for working with difficulty, and provides an intelligent framework for containing our deep-seated fear about coping with what life brings, especially as the end of the game nears.

In my case, the sea and time wash away my anxiety somewhat. Walking helps, a cup of tea helps. Doing what I can to alleviate my difficulty helps. I tell my son I am not coping with the dog thing. He relents and says the dog can sleep in the bed with me. Dear little hot water bottle dog. Now we are both happier. I shift rooms and sleep in a cosier place. I make soup. Cooking soothes me. I sit in the garden in the sun, watching the wattlebirds. I soften into my body and don't let my mind run amok with bad scenarios. I start to enjoy the house, the adventure, my granddaughter's art supplies. It is rare for me to have times in the day when I deeply know that there is nothing the matter. I make daily effort to notice these times, to savour them, to not take them for granted. Whatever I nurture will flourish. There are no tigers here, I tell myself. Today is big enough to contain everything, and I am safe and it is good to be alive.

SEPTEMBER: ON WONDER

May I appreciate this precious life.

Spring has well and truly arrived. Warm days, blossoms aplenty, summery clothes to be washed and worn, wildflowers of brilliant beauty, a desire to clean things.

Yet I have misplaced my sense of wonder lately. I seem to be addicted to my own negative thinking, like Eeyore with his usual gloomy spin.

All is not lost. Along with other beneficial mind states, such as gratitude, generosity and compassion, wonder can be cultivated.

First up, when you think about it, the fact that these particular atoms came together in this particular order so that we can be alive is a total miracle. It should not be taken for granted. Yet we do. How often we trudge through our days, forgetting to bow down to the marvel of our own existence within the wider miracle with a sense of please and thank you.

I'm making daily effort to find life less of an effort and to cultivate wonder, for surely loving kindness to myself requires loving my life and enjoying it while I can. All too soon, the king and the pawn will end up in the same box, as the Italian proverb reminds us.

Wondering involves a sense of inquiry. Life is an experiment. Living with open-minded curiosity gives life a zesty, merry flavour. When in doubt, lean towards awesome.

There will still be trouble, strife, crazy people who do terrifying things. There will still be corrupt politicians and dog-shit days, but focusing on these things is not the only game in town. If we walk in beauty, taking delight in the mystery, rather than being ground down by the shadowy and difficult, this outlook becomes a habit of mind.

You don't have to look far to find the strange amazingness of people and life, when you set forth with eyes of wow. Let us appreciate and be dazzled by the richness of our everyday existence.

'I can see your penis underwater,' a laughing kid yells at her brother in the swimming pool. Having fun and being silly is an art, a wonderment readily and always available.

'Nana Brigie, Nana Brigie, I've got a wiggly tooth!' My granddaughter runs towards me, joyous with the thrill of it. I've never seen a happier child.

Another day, she's telling me about a boy in her class at school who likes to play at fighting zombies. I am in the other room drying dishes and not quite listening properly, but I sense it's troubling her.

'Zombies aren't real,' I say encouragingly. 'What else isn't real? Are unicorns real?'

I love these conversations. Through her eyes I see the world afresh. I dread the day when she tells me fairies and mermaids are not real.

'No,' she says, a little doubtfully. Shortly afterwards she goes into the other room where her dress-ups are kept. 'Don't come in!' she instructs firmly.

When I'm given the royal command to enter, there she is, on all fours, with a unicorn headdress on, and a twinkle in her eye, demonstrating beyond a doubt that unicorns are real. She then does a little unicorn dance for me, up on her hooves. Bless that unicorn child.

◇◇◇◇◇◇◇◇

Children are a great source of wonder. For a start, babies. The fact that a person grows inside another person and comes out screaming, breathing and alive is itself beyond miraculous. From then on, wonder begins. The first taste of mango, the first experience of the sea, the first anything, everything new and bright. In Zen this is called beginner's mind, a way of seeing things as if for the first time, knowing them to be extraordinary.

◇◇◇◇◇◇◇◇

A list of recent wonderments:

Container ships with lovely names: *Dream Beauty* and *Destiny Ace.*

A long aisle of products for cats in the two-dollar shop. Who knew, and lucky cats.

A Middle Eastern recipe involving a fish which the chef kept swimming in grape juice, in order to enhance its flavour, before cooking.

Rainbow lorikeets, swooping by, a swift flash of miraculous colour.

Swamp hens at the lake, strutting around, elegant and awkward at the same time.

The University of Bristol spent $35,000 finding a new name for one of their buildings. After a lengthy consultancy process and two hundred suggestions, they narrowed it down to the top five, took a vote and kept the old name.

◇◇◇◇◇◇◇◇

Let us love our lives. Let us be astonished by them. Let us savour the small pleasures and give ourselves over to amazement and delight.

OCTOBER: SOLITUDE AND CONNECTION

May I enjoy being with others.
May I enjoy being alone.

Very agreeable weather. Clear skies. After Too Cold and before Too Hot. Frocks, necklaces, earrings, sitting in the sun. Lighter linen on my bed: purple with spring flowers.

I've been looking at intimacy and solitude. It's interesting territory. Having been married for thirty years, to two different men, I know a little about being part of a couple. I was single for years when my last marriage ended, and after the initial crunch I came to terms with being alone.

Then this recent ride on the merry-go-round of love with all its ups and downs and sideways. Partnership doesn't get any easier when one is older. Harder, perhaps, because personalities and habits have become crusty, entrenched.

Anyhow, I am alone again, and facing what this means to me.

In the newspaper I read that after ending a significant relationship it takes four years to regain one's former state of ease and equanimity. This is both encouraging and discouraging. It means I feel less weird about still feeling weird about the relationship ending. It also means I have three years, one month, six hours and seventeen minutes until I'll feel good again. Patience is a virtue, so I am told. Actually, I'm pretty happy, most of the time.

Solitude and loneliness are not the same thing. Solitude is enjoying being alone. It provides sustenance and inner richness, and is peaceful and refreshing. Loneliness is different. It's a universal human emotion but quite hard to define. Loneliness involves feeling isolated, disconnected, our needs unmet by our social relationships. Without a sense of belonging, or being seen and valued by others, we can feel sad, bitter, vulnerable.

As with most things, balance is important. It is good to spend time with ourselves. It is good to spend time with others. Some people are better at being alone. Like many writers, I lean towards enjoying my own company, but like every other bugger on the planet, sometimes I am really lonely.

Some folk thrive on group contact. It energises them.

Some find it overwhelming, confusing and draining. I like being with one or two people but I don't often enjoy parties, for example. Once this bothered me. Now I accept it. I give group events my best shot and sometimes surprise myself by having a good time, but my long-time habit is to have an immediate shame attack on the way home about getting it wrong somehow: talking too much or forgetting to say goodbye to someone. I now accept this will happen and remind myself not to punish myself this way. Instead I put on the kettle, put on my dressing gown and relax.

My most valued relationships are with my family, beloved every one of them, and with my friends, truly glorious people without whom my life would not be worth living.

In *Lost Connections*, Johann Hari's great book about depression, he stresses the need for connection with self, with tribe, with society, with culture, with meaningful work, with other people. To this end, once a week I shelve books at a local eco-community centre, where I'm forging some interesting connections with the other volunteers. Making sure I have human contact every day and engaging with people is important but it's a juggling act, and it can be a tricky one.

What is it that makes being with people challenging for

me? Mainly it's anxiety. Am I saying the wrong thing? Is the other person finding me annoying, weird, controlling, idiotic? Well, maybe and maybe not, but when I recognise and accept my social anxiety, it frees me up and things go better.

Loving kindness to me is reminding myself that I am okay. When I feel good about myself, more love and kindness is available for others. Sometimes I do a check-in, in my journal or in my head. How connected am I feeling with myself? How connected am I feeling with other people? Aiming for balance, knowing it won't be perfect. Sometimes it will be life with a capital F whatever I do. Permission to get things wrong. Permission to pick myself up, apologise if need be, start afresh.

Letting go of judgment is important. We're unique, and we see all things differently. It doesn't make anyone right or wrong. When other people behave in challenging ways, I aim to have a heart big enough to contain it. When people act badly they're probably feeling shitty, so I make like the Buddha and try to love them anyway. Sometimes it works.

In my journey towards becoming who I'd like to be when I grow up, I'm also learning to stay out of other people's stuff. My world is immediately easier, both in practical terms and in terms of my own emotional steadiness. I've wasted a lot of time trying to fix and control other people but I have finally learned the elusive yet obvious truth that I don't have the power to make everything all better for anyone else. When I figure out what belongs to me and what doesn't, life lightens up considerably.

Jean-Paul Sartre famously said that hell is other people. For me, hell can be myself. Like many others, I've spent a lifetime feeling unacceptable, an outsider, awkward, shy, crazy, fat, wrong in some way. It's a hard game to give up but author and teacher Byron Katie has observed that it is nobody else's job to like us, just our own. More and more I am worrying less about being liked and putting that energy into liking myself. It feels soft, and very spacious.

NOVEMBER: LIVING SIMPLY

I have enough. I am enough.

Ryokan was a haiku poet, calligrapher and Zen monk in the eighteenth century who was well known for living quietly and simply. I joke that I am the Ryokan of Shenton Park, because my priority is to live quietly and simply.

In contemporary capitalist society, this can feel like swimming against the stream but I'm not alone in believing that creating a simple life is a worthy aspiration. So many people are realising that more is not always better, and are making efforts to walk the talk of this. My old friends Dave and Annie believed that if you didn't want something before you saw it advertised, you didn't need it. They had chooks and a goat, orange peel drying on the woodstove to scent their home. Tiny houses, the slow food movement, buy-nothing sites, recycling centres, op shops, verge shopping—these are all good evidence of efforts being made to make do with less.

I am enough, I have enough is a particularly useful mantra to invoke when tempted to buy more objects, clothes or fancy foods in an effort to soothe the soul. No amount of shopping truly helps with emptiness, loneliness or sorrow. Better to face these emotions and allow them to come and to go. No need to spend any dollarbucks and, ultimately, it's liberating.

I like the Japanese word *ōryōki,* which means 'enoughness'. There is a world of difference between need and want. When I let wanting arrive and rest awhile but do not satisfy it, it soon goes away. But when I respond to wanting with getting, the satisfaction is often short-lived. Wanting then goes looking for something else to want. This does not mean I can never have ice-cream. It means that I don't have ice-cream every time I want it, and that's okay by me.

This month, with temperatures and tempers rising, and Christmas tills already ringing, I'm considering what is enough, so I can live simply in a world that constantly lures me in a different direction.

What am I prepared to let go of, in order to live more simply and peacefully?

The list is long.

Shopping as recreation. Trying to impress others with the stuff I have. Restaurant dining, except for special occasions. Constant hurrying. Worrying. Having to be good. Wanting to be perfect. Trying to please. Overworking. Zoning out. Getting lost in thought and indulging in endless discursive thinking. Needing to be right. Needing to be appreciated. Needing to be in control. Holding grudges. Getting hooked into other people's stuff. Putting energy into relationships that no longer work. Negative rumination. Living by shoulds and musts.

Letting go, letting be, moving forward, moving on.

How am I walking my own talk to create a simple, quiet life?

I'm eating slowly, appreciatively and mindfully. I am slowing down my walking, talking and decision-making.

I am simplifying my finances and saving heaps of money by not trying to impress people. I don't go shopping as a diversion, and I don't shop when I am tired, hungry or sad. Zen teacher Reb Anderson once said the essence of Zen was to stop shopping. Insight teacher Joseph Goldstein tells a story about walking down Fifth Avenue, his mind consumed by wanting things, and how unpleasant it felt, compared to a different occasion on which he strolled along the same street, admiring things and enjoying them but not wanting them. (This is not just hippy-trippy bullshit. Endless striving to make more money to buy more things has serious repercussions for health, both mental and physical.)

I am taking good care of what I do have. I am polishing my shoes, getting my car serviced, mending my clothes. When practical, I do things myself rather than hiring someone to do it. Cleaning my car with a bucket of soapy water and a hose is good exercise, for example. I'm growing my own herbs, and using the art supplies I have instead of buying more. I'm giving away clothes that don't fit, knick-knacks that don't mean much, kitchen equipment I rarely use, books I won't read again.

I'm using what I have, the groceries in my cupboards and the food in my fridge, to make delicious meals. I'm wearing what I already own, and am amazed at what I already have in my wardrobe, and how good it looks when creatively combined.

When I need a larger item, I go to Gumtree first. I don't buy new if I don't have to. When I need to buy new, I research first, ensuring that the intended purchase is ecologically sound and decently made. 'Buy cheap, buy twice' is my accountant's advice, and worth considering.

I've been pretending that I have a tattoo on my wrist saying *Get Less*, surrounded by a tiny moon and stars.

Although imaginary and invisible, it's a guiding light. Loving kindness to self can't be separated from loving kindness to the planet. Taking care of oneself by living simply is a profound act, both personal and political.

DECEMBER: CREATIVITY

I vow to live creatively, softly, kindly.

I like Christmas. Ignoring the commercial crap, I give the season my all. It's a time of getting together, of making cards and gifts and edible delights. It's summer and beach and salads and ice-cream and falling asleep under a tree. It's wearing bright colours, hats, sparkly jewels. It's the season to celebrate and make merry, to hang out with beloveds, raising a teacup to mystery and magic, enchantment, divinity and delight.

My year of loving kindness to myself is nearly over. I've come a long way since I began making a conscious daily effort to be good to myself. Shame and non-acceptance are not running my show the way they used to. Life feels softer, sweeter. I've learned that I don't have to apologise for being myself, and that when I treat myself with tenderness I am stronger and happier.

Seeds have been planted; however, the tree of me will

need kind watering from now until forever because she is still there—the neglected girl sent to school with unbrushed hair, the frightened child whose father killed himself, the kid whose mother drank too much. The one who trudges, who just gets by. The baffled one. The sad person. The witchy critic. These parts of me live alongside the strong woman, the funny one, the smart one, the loving mother, the joyous grandmother, the loyal friend, the dreamer, the seeker, the optimist, the writer. It's quite a circus in there sometimes, yet I know the way forward. To stop thinking of myself as a fix-it project. To live beyond the labels. To not consolidate the self as a fixed position. Instead, to inhabit each moment fully, to be contented, to live in a simple, generous way, to appreciate the goodness around me, to stand steady in the face of difficulty.

More and more I trust that creativity and rest are my best medicines, that play is the highest form of research, as Einstein said. Creativity requires me to be open to my inner life, to allow ambiguity, to trust myself and my process. Creativity invites me to dress colourfully, to sew and draw and cook, to visit the beach and the park, to practise doing lovely things which are necessary for my healthy survival. It lies beyond seeking security, approval, comfort and control.

Under the surface of duty and habit are fresh ways of being and doing. It's big wisdom to examine something carefully and realise that if it brings you trouble, stop doing it. This includes negative self-talk, mean-spirited behaviour, grabbing more than you need, hanging out with people who bring you down, any behaviour that exploits or demeans others, anything that wears you out or drains you.

Starting from a place of self-acceptance, moving outwards into a world that badly needs love and good energy. Extending the hand of truth, integrity and kindness to others is a deep form of self-compassion. Although we do not always see our place in the great mystery, we are not separate. We are our mother's recipes, our neighbour's sorrow, our friend's memories, our dog's friskiness. We are the last cigarette we ever smoked, the first heart we ever broke, the fireworks, the folly, the shoe abandoned at the beach. All of this is connected in ways we will never fully understand but here we are, in this beautiful broken world with our tender aching hearts, a part of something vast and magnificent. To trust life as it is, and savour one's part in it, what could be lovelier or kinder than that?

It has been quite a year. The things I have lived I share with you. Let us give the Buddha the last word, which always seems a wise thing to do. *You can search the ten-fold universe and not find a single person more worthy of loving kindness than yourself.*

ON NEW YEAR'S EVE, A PRAYER

May I make way for the new, greeting every moment as a fresh beginning.

May I be truly content with the abundance of life. May I let things be as they are, say *Yes Please* to everything and all of it, write *Heart's Ease* in cloud letters in the wide blue sky. May I trust in the wide magic of everyday existence, imagine positive outcomes instead of bothering everything to death.

May I encourage myself at all times.

May I remember to live creatively, luxuriating in the simple, the quiet and the miraculously ordinary.

May I connect. May I help others when I have authentic energy for it and rest when I don't. May I remember that I am a part of something much larger than myself, and act accordingly.

May the politicians forgo their own greed for power and money for the sake of all beings, for the sake of the broken world.

Can there please be a section in the newspaper called Poetry instead of one called Property.

I would also like some green velvet slippers with roses on.

Namaste. Thank you. Amen.

UNABLE TO SAVE THE MANY BEINGS

I am sorry, Dipa Ma.
When you visited America you remarked
that people do not need nine types of tea.
I'm ashamed to tell you
how many sorts of tea I have.

Lord Buddha, I apologise.
Despite your teachings
I often remain entangled
in useless preoccupations.

I bow down before you, Zen masters.
Greed, hatred and ignorance
rise endlessly in me.
I create my own confusion.

Please forgive me, Kuan Yin,
for acting like a complete bozo
much of the time.

Yet this evening, at dusk,
lorikeets in the singing gum trees,
my life suddenly a blessing
of its own accord.
I raise my teacup in your honour,
oh teachers who have led the way.

ON JOURNALS, NOTEBOOKS, DIARIES AND ME

Cats like to prowl, dogs like to sniff, and writers love to write. Words are what we do and what we love.

We write anywhere: on serviettes and old envelopes, in the dust on the back of a car window. If we could, we'd write *my heart is broken* in skywriting, then later replace it with *precious tender heart* because it sounded better.

Once I almost wrote *Help* on a whiteboard at a Zen retreat, even though it would have been inappropriate.

The writer's mind is very mysterious. Fragments and thoughts arrive by themselves, elusive, easily forgotten.

Thus, notebooks.

Our lives are messy, dreadful, bewildering, beautiful; our journey is our own. Writing about it can help us make sense of it, stay in touch with it.

Thus, journals.

When I was six, I carefully copied out lines of poetry,

gathered wisdoms and things that interested me into a small brown hardcover notebook. Sixty years later, I'm still at it. I keep a traditional diary of sorts, a personal record of my life and times. Sometimes I'm given a fancy journal for Christmas, but many of my journals are the plain Chinese ones which are cheap and easily available. My entries are sporadic, and peppered with Buddhist quotes and small drawings. This creative space is a site of reflection where I complain, enjoy, document and process my world for my own edification. I believe that anything which provides insight into my life will also provide insight into the human condition and feed into my writing. This process is a strange thing, operating in ways not immediately apparent.

I have another, larger, hardback lined book which is a more writerly journal, in which to collect and store writing ideas, random lines to use some day, other people's insights about writing, and newspaper clippings. My latest strange clipping is about a $425 high-tech mirror which gives a detailed analysis of the most unattractive parts of your own face on a daily basis. I'm not intending to buy one.

Lastly, I have a travelling notebook in my handbag for snippets of overheard conversation and brilliant thoughts which arrive in a café or on the train, and float dreamily away if they are not scribbled down.

Everyone has their own system. Some put everything in

one place, others have various notebooks or journals on the go at any one time. Some use pen and paper, others their phone or laptop. Methods may shapeshift over time. Experiment. Try blank pages if lined pages feel confined. Go bigger, use colour, write at a different time of day or in new locations.

Writer and teacher Julia Cameron suggests 'morning pages' as one of three vital writing tools, the other two being daily walking and weekly artistic dates. Buy the cheapest school exercise book you can find, then write madly every morning, or in the evening if you prefer. Write freely. Avoid trying to be impressive, literary or coherent. Just let your mind flow onto the page. It is an excellent way to loosen up, unblock your creative energy and re-establish a sense of enjoyment in the land of pen and thought, or even better, in your life. When you stop trying to be right or clever, and allow the psyche to speak, amazing things may happen. Writing lists in journals can be a lot of fun. Try these:

Things I Once Believed

Lovely Places to Eat a Mango

Things An Adult Should Not Say To A Child

Zen author Natalie Goldberg suggests we re-read our old journals, reflecting on where we've been and where we thought we were headed. We discover parts of ourselves:

age-old neuroses, early adventures, forgotten thoughts. Recently I got out a box of old journals, spanning over twenty years, and am slowly reading and digesting them.

I learn that I have always been sad in autumn, that I have always found writing difficult, that people say they will love each other forever and mean it at the time but later change their minds. I learn that I have struggled with every book I've ever written yet they've all turned out okay. I see that I grapple with conflicting desires for solitude and human connection. I rediscover wisdom from dead poets, past gurus, live friends. In 2007 my friend Brett said, 'There is nothing to believe in. There is no faith, no belief required. It all just is.' I don't think I heard him properly then, but I'm listening now.

I remember nothing at all about Christmas 2003 but on Boxing Day I wrote: *Xmas over. Thank God. Absolutely shattered.*

In New York, a small bar in Brooklyn is famous for a cocktail named God's Daisy Chain, composed of gin, Aperol and sparkling wine. I noted it in case I could use that information somewhere some day, and now I have.

By traversing the oceans of my past, I learn that my preoccupations have always been the same and my game plan is still current: stay in the moment, live simply, stop worrying about the way it isn't.

Journalling can be a tool for awakening, a sacred act, a pleasure, a way to access and enjoy the depths of your own wisdom, particularly if you are sad, stale, lost or creatively malnourished. Don't bother angsting over whether journalling is a psychological pastime or a sensible creative tool, because creativity, spiritual life and personal growth are intimately entwined and whatever nourishes one will feed the other. Grab that pen.

ON FRIDAY

It's autumn but the weather has lost its way. After an endless summer, finally, a little rain. Mugginess, uncertainty, my neighbour's breakfast: fried onion, burnt toast.

Downstairs, a woman plays the piano with stumbling passion. I'm flooded with an overwhelming love of the world, despite yet another friend nearing death, despite the continuing planetary turmoil, despite my ancient fears.

'Today,' I say to myself, 'today I must do some writing.' Then I vacuum my apartment, make lentil soup and rearrange my wardrobe. Writers don't want to write, they want to have written.

I spend some pleasant time inventing a fictional world, somewhat like Japan except different. In this land there is a Realm of Books and Inkwells, a Courtyard of Lingering Moonbeams, a Pavilion of Strange Forgettings and a Tower of Alphabets and Teapots. In this land my name is Kimono

Morning Star and this whole thing leads me nowhere in particular but gets me as far as morning tea. The main tools of a writer: the long walk and the hot beverage.

Next, I google around for a bit. Avoiding writing is an all-day pursuit and takes skill and perseverance. Who knew that today is Good Riddance Day? Apparently one should take an object or an idea one would like to leave behind and destroy it by shredding, burying or setting it on fire. I am not quite sure how to shred, bury or set an idea on fire but it has a certain appeal and I would definitely do it if I wasn't busy choosing between redoing my toenails or visiting the shops to buy cheese.

I spend more time wondering how come I thought I had twenty dollars in my wallet but now I don't and I absolutely can't remember spending it but obviously I did unless someone snuck into my purse and stole it, which seems unlikely, except I really, really can't remember spending it ...

Then on to worrying about why X has not returned my text. Usually it turns out the person is just busy but there is plenty of mileage to be had from angsting about the fact that they neither like nor respect me and how rude and etc., etc., etc. Their friendly text, when it comes, is a blessing.

Back to work, I tell myself, and get busy looking at the blank screen, blankly. Tis busy work, being a writer. What did the writer do in the morning? Shifted a comma. What did the writer do in the afternoon? Shifted it back again.

I wander around my apartment complex, avoiding writing and looking at the gardens. Some residents have healthy herb gardens and some do not. I run into a friend and we speak about poor sleep, magnesium, acupuncture and her latest op shop score, a cheerful pink coat. She's come from a meeting that she says was 'confrontative'. Although invented, her word is a marvellous word, just as serviceable as 'confrontational'.

At lunchtime I read the paper. Plenty of bad news. A restaurant review mentions a menu item of 'charred corn with burnt bacon'. Really? If I wanted burnt food, I could stay home and burn it myself. This would save heaps.

In the afternoon I write a little, rest a little, prepare some food. There is something very soothing about peeling apples and rubbing butter into oats. In error, I succumb to an eensy-weensy moment of self-pity over the love affair that ended clumsily. It was a mistake made from loneliness. William Holden said something like this in *Love Is a Many-Splendored Thing*, and he was right.

At afternoon tea time I sit in the sun and paint my toenails a charming shade called 'Spice of Life', then add a glittery layer. Bling is always good. Next I visit my neighbour to see if he has any old *New Yorker*s for me. He hasn't. He mentions a thing his mother used to say.

'Take the opporchancity, Ron.'

I love that. I say it over and over. *Take the opporchancity.*

Another friend once told me her mother used to cheer her up when things went wrong by saying, 'Never mind, Perle. Another trolley will come along soon.' I start thinking about New York, where she was raised, and find myself watching an eight-minute video about the last trolleys in Brooklyn. They ran on wires, looked a lot like buses, and stopped operating in 1956, in case you're interested.

My mother used to say '*festina lente*', which means 'hurry slowly' in Latin. This is handy in a retrospective way. For example, when you spill something all over the kitchen because you were hurrying fast you can reflect upon the fact that you should have hurried slower. My mother also used to say 'I hope you know what you're doing'. I didn't.

At five pm I stroll around the lake. A woman walking two little poodles smiles at me and says, 'Good morning.' She looks quite normal. However, one of us is wrong about what time of day it is.

I have written very little today but it has been a good day. I'm happy and I like Fridays.

ON DEATH

When Amber was dying, she was surrounded by goodness because all her life she had gathered goodness. Her dying was peaceful and inspiring but now she is gone. Gone forever, gone somewhere else and we don't know where. I keep wanting to email her, post her *New Yorker* cartoons as I always did. My beloved niece will never be here again. Her five years with brain cancer have come to an end. Her husband is stumbling. Her son is fifteen years old. Those of us who loved her struggle to find meaning, onwards we go, on unsteady feet, through our ordinary days.

Summer. I am here but one day I will not be. Amber is gone. The rest of us to follow.

'Sparkly is a Christmas colour,' says my granddaughter. She is my happy place, but I am in the dark land of grief now, deeply sad. Other people's problems annoy me; they seem so trivial. I'm irritable, tired, weepy, borderline depressed. I try to write helpful things to my grieving family, faking wisdom I don't quite have.

There is a difference between wanting to live and being scared of dying. Amber wasn't scared of dying, but she wanted to live. Her death has left a rent in the fabric of our family. She was the queen of baking, wrote excellent haiku, loved playing Scrabble. Her hands were delicate. Her intelligence was fierce. I do not want her to be gone.

Death is the one truth we don't want to know about. We think it won't happen to us, but it will. We don't want it to happen to those we love, but it does.

At the palliative care workshop I went to later for my own benefit, they told us we have to have 'the conversation' with our nearest kin about what we would like regarding our dying. Sensible stuff like wills and end-of-life instructions and funerals.

My son is not in the least bit keen to have this conversation with me. I am not sure if it is because he is too busy or because he doesn't want to think about his mother dying. Probably both.

I tell him which songs I'd like at my funeral.

'I've written them down,' I say. 'There's a list in a folder, along with bank details and other important stuff, like how to arrange an eco-funeral.'

'You'll be dead, Mum. I get to pick the songs.'

We laugh and get on with our living, but one day he will have to pick the songs for my funeral, or I will have to help pick his, and this will seem a dreadful thing whichever way the cards fall.

Death is the greatest mystery of all. We do not know who will be next, or how they will go. What happens after we die? No-one knows that either, although there are plenty of theories. For some, religion has answered the question with certainty, for others there is no certainty at all.

Meanwhile, we have a life to live. All of this for a short time only, as my Zen teacher says. Amber is gone. Meanwhile, there is the day, the moment. There is the beach, the teapot, the fading dusk, the bird singing, the child colouring in.

ON THINGS TO DO WHEN LIFE GOES SIDEWAYS

Stay in your pyjamas.
Compile a list of your favourite goddesses.
Send blessings to beggars.
Buy flowers for someone. The someone can be you.
Adopt a meerkat. Or a unicorn.
Spend the day without a plan.
Name your houseplants.
Eat toast with marmalade, and maybe a pear.
Act your age, which today is seven.
Try a new café. Wear a new outfit. Find a new hat.
Dance around the living room.
Draw a picture of the things you love.
Sit in a tree. Plant a tree. Talk to a tree.
Make paper dolls. Give them fancy hats and plenty of buttons.
If anyone asks your name, say Eloise.
For lunch, pancakes, soup or whatever the hell you like.
Go to bed early, with a pile of good books.

ON FRIENDSHIP

Apparently, once upon a time, back in the day, under a tree, Venerable Ananda, one of the Buddha's top disciples, commented that good friends were half of the holy life. One would imagine he'd get an affirmative, but the Buddha disagreed, in his usual kind, loving, Buddha manner.

'Don't say that, Ananda. Don't say that. Admirable friendship, admirable companionship, admirable camaraderie is actually the whole of the holy life,' the Buddha replied, going on to explain that wise friends keep you on the right path, inclining you towards a noble life by their speech and actions. He also said that if you wrap rotten fish in sweet grass, the grass will begin to stink, meaning that it is best not to mix with fools.

Good friends are a great blessing. They are people you could call at two am. Knowing that is a gift, even though you do not ring them at two am. Decent friends behave with integrity and authenticity, supporting you in your sanity and not abandoning you in your madness. They wholeheartedly celebrate your triumphs and pardon your fiascos. Good friends are respectful of your time and honour their arrangements. A true friend can tell you a hard and necessary truth without shaming you.

Different friendships provide different things. I have dharma friends, writer friends, café friends, friends in other lands, a friend who has been a wise mentor in times of difficulty.

What sort of a friend am I? Loyal, creative and generous, I hope. I aim to be a good listener but sometimes I butt in excitedly or give unsolicited advice. I will possibly be working on improving these bad habits for the next three lifetimes.

All friendships contain ebb and flow, but sometimes friendships end. They dwindle and fade, or explode in angry fireworks. A major blow-up can sometimes be mended but sometimes it can't. Having known each other for a long time is not enough. A friendship needs to have current common ground, be a meeting of minds, and feel safe. People who make themselves feel better by making you feel worse are unsuitable friends. People locked into endless complaint are draining, and supporting them in this behaviour does not help them change. Letting go of an old friendship can be a relief or it can be very hard.

Sometimes we see our own part in the situation, and can let go with a measure of grace and wisdom. In this way, it is important to be a friend to ourself. Most friendships wax and wane over time, but the best ones continue. If there are difficulties we may need to talk things over but often, if we keep our mouth shut and our heart open, things come right by themselves. It is wise to remember that everyone has their own unfolding and that the way we see things is only one way of seeing things. I imagine even the Buddha and Ananda had off moments in their friendship, and so will we.

ONWARDS

On the fifth day of Christmas: vow to be your own true love.
On your birthday: be happy. The alternative to being alive is to be dead.
On dignity and nobility: cultivate.
On your deathbed: be glad of everything and breathe easy.
On other people: cut them plenty of slack.
On really idiotic people: show compassion, or avoid.
On the telephone: listen carefully. Don't butt in.
On anxiety: remember, one day none of it will matter.
On the table: books, pens, diary, flowers, cards, stamps, envelopes, lists.
On computers: read the screen and try not to panic.
On poetry: read it, breathe it, live it.
On hospital: eat the food, smile a lot. They'll let you out sooner.
On letting go: quite difficult. Easier to let be.
On clothing: comfortable, colourful, recycled.

On op shops: give to them, buy from them.
On dancing: do plenty.
On fruit and vegetables: eat plenty.
On activity: do less. Savour more.
On living simply: unplug as much as possible. Don't make shopping a hobby. Eat what's in the fridge.
On toast: mushrooms. Tomatoes. Cheese. Marmalade. Almond Butter. Avocado and feta. Homemade beans in spicy sauce. A portrait of Jesus. Whatever you like.

ON SOLACE

Sad is one of my expert areas. Sad persons are not unusual in my family. My tribe are creative, interesting, intelligent and, in the main, good cooks, but we are keenly in touch with human melancholy. If you also sometimes feel that life is a losing game, allow me to share some encouraging words.

The first thing to tell you is that you are not alone. Sad is a normal human emotion, along with happy, scared, cranky, anxious, disappointed, hopeful, bored and many other feelings, all of which are entirely normal, except for murderous rage which is not to be encouraged.

Making friends with your emotions is wise. Feelings arrive, fed by causes and conditions, and sooner than you think they float away like clouds. It is good to welcome them with open arms and a kind heart, particularly the most difficult ones. This sounds easy but it is not. When you are really struggling with sadness, take heart. There are many beneficial things you can do.

Walk. It will bring you into your body, into the sunshine, into the day. Walking reminds you that there are camellias, cats, bicycles and birds; that the universe is bigger than your skull and skin; that every ordinary thing is a miracle to behold.

Journal. Write it down. Draw pictures to go with the words. Write letters you wish you could send, then burn them. The page is a safe container and writing is a place of insight and comfort.

Learn to challenge your gloomy negative thinking, not following it into dark and dangerous places. This takes grit and practice but you do have agency. Strengthen the neural pathways that lead to happy.

Watch funny shows. Mix with cheerful people. Sing in a choir, in the car, anywhere except perhaps in the psychiatrist's waiting room. Find the things you love, and do more of them. Make each day a pleasure garden.

Do something every day that brings ease to your body: yoga, tai chi, running, swimming, strolling, hugs, dancing, gardening. Feeling easy in the body really helps the mind. No doubt there is a sound scientific reason for this but for now, take my word for it.

Talk. To your mother, your cousin, your dog. Being heard and held with kindness by another living being is healing. If things are really tough, consult a health professional. Listen to your inner wisdom and don't be too proud to get help when you need it.

Antidepressants can provide a short-term answer to lift you out of a hole that feels too deep to climb out of by yourself. Medications have side effects, though, and are not an instant or a total cure.

Avoid things that temporarily mask sadness but may increase it: recreational drugs, alcohol, binge eating, endless television. Hanging out with negative, self-absorbed people is a downer, as is focusing on fearful media spin.

When anxiety or panic set in, come home to the safe harbours of breath, bodily sensations, sounds and sensory contact.

When you are feeling really low is the most important time for self-compassion and self-care. Kind self-talk and many treats are good medicine.

Sometimes it helps to see the bigger picture. You are alive. Don't take this for granted. Your breath is still flowing in and out, and your breakfast still tastes good. The world is big and wide and you are a part of it. Life is a fleeting thing, sometimes so elegant and simple, sometimes a dark horse we don't know how to ride.

Even though total satisfaction is unavailable in this life, there are still penguins, cucumbers, palm trees, grandfathers, babies, toast and stardust, the divinely ordinary, the ordinarily divine. Grant yourself full permission to be who you are, no longer struggling, in harmony with reality, with things as they are.

In the words of my friend and zen teacher Arthur Wells: May your body be at ease. May your heart be happy. May your feet be steady on the ground.

And remember, there's only a week between a bad haircut and a good one.

ON WALKING

Walking is soul medicine. It is good for your body, too. It is air and street and foot and flower and garden and stride. It is amble, shamble, shuffle, trudge, skip, meander, wander. Walking is a time when ideas arrive, lungs breathe, and if you're lucky, your troubles are left behind. It is one of the many things we take for granted, until we can no longer do it.

Walking is a way to enter the day, the world. It is a way to escape yourself, to find yourself, to discover that, as Jack Kerouac said, there is nowhere to go but everywhere and, as Steven Wright noted, everywhere is within walking distance if you have the time.

I've walked through tropical-scented hotel gardens in Bali, on lonely beaches in New Zealand, along the bustling sidewalks of New York. On a hillside near Firenze I wandered down a sunlit alley and came across a plaque above a modest doorway saying *Galileo was born here.*

I've walked in school shoes, bare feet, ancient sneakers, red sandals and purple suede boots. Once upon a time I walked away from my old life in my falling-to-bits shoes. There are still a few places my feet would like to go.

There's something serendipitous about not quite knowing where you're going. Down the street of blowsy roses? Towards the lake? Do you have the energy for a long walk, for a brisk trot to the library, or are you only up for a short excursion to the shop to buy tomatoes, and maybe some chocolate.

I'm writing about walking. I'm stuck. I need a break, so I go walking.

Green grapefruit, ripening. Speckled leaves, falling. Camellias. Cool autumn sun. Two delicious guavas, fallen from a tree. Roses with real rose fragrance. The deep beauty of a quiet afternoon. I realise what to do about a tricky situation with a friend. I magically remember something that had been eluding me. I return happier about my day, my everything. Many great ideas arrive when one is walking.

In New Zealand there's a thing called a *green prescription*, which doctors try before resorting to medication for depression. It advocates healthy eating and simple physical activity, such as walking, to improve health in every way: sleep, mood, stronger bones, lower blood pressure, reduced arthritis pain and many other benefits. Such a simple and good thing to do. Hippocrates was right. Walking is indeed the best medicine.

Walking meditation is another lovely thing, a gentle calming practice, as easy as staying current and staying in your feet as you walk from your car to the supermarket, instead of getting lost in anxious thinking. Vietnamese Zen monk Thich Nhat Hanh teaches the practice of walking meditation and suggests we walk mindfully, as if our feet are kissing the earth.

Walking with a friend is excellent. It is a great pleasure to walk with someone, talking at leisure.

Walking with a child is a treat. I love walking with my granddaughter in the park beside her house. Together we have walked as fairies, mermaids, babies, rabbits.

'Sometimes I just need to hold hands,' she once said, and so we did.

Walking alone is a fine thing. So is walking with a dog. Or with other people, children and various dogs. Walking is uncomplicated. It is travelling magic. One foot in front of the other, enjoying every step.

A FEW OF MY DREAMS

A dream of a lost button. A dream of a silver button.
A dream of a tin of buttons.
A dream about a pair of talking underpants.
A dream of adopting four children, then giving one back.
A dream of twigs in the hair. The more twigs I wear in my hair the more everyone likes me.
A dream I am very glad to wake up from.
A dream of finding money. A dream of losing money.
A dream of using jelly beans instead of money.
A dream that makes me feel as if there's a right answer to everything and I almost know what it is.
A dream too deep to remember.

ON SINGAPORE

It smelled of roses in Singapore. It was my first visit. Nothing was as I imagined.

Nowhere ever is, but I came to like it: Little India, Chinatown, cheap taxis, delicious oily *murtabak*, the pool at the hotel, the tropical night air, orchids, sweet chai in the noisy food hall. I gathered modest treasures: tiny statues of deities, incense, paper ephemera to be burnt as offerings for the dead to use in heaven—pictures of cosmetics, cars, whisky, clothing, cigarettes, high-heeled shoes. You might need these things, for you are a long time dead.

In Singapore it was the end of us. Everything you did bothered me. What bothered me most was how little I liked myself when I was with you. I wish I had been able to love you more. You deserved a good love affair. But in the end I didn't even like you much. I certainly didn't like the me I was with you: controlling, critical, changeable, impatient, confused.

I escaped on small adventures by myself. At the Chinese Buddhist temple, amongst fake lotus, real chrysanthemums and a thousand gilded Buddhas, I bowed down three times, so much sadness in my heart. I was a stranger to delight, a stranger to myself.

Coming out after monsoon rain, I find my sodden shoes are wrecked.

Life is one long grieving.

When my mother left my father, he killed himself. This did not give me a whole lot of permission to leave a man.

◇◇◇◇◇◇◇◇◇

I wait until we return to Perth, then end the relationship, finally, after trying to do so many times. Initially you are bewildered. Later, angry. This I cannot fix for you.

Time passes. At first I am not much happier, burdened with regret, confusion, loneliness, longing. What a mess. It's not just us I am mourning, it is all the losses of my life. People are not very good at letting go, but in the end, we have to. Every day, every death, every worry or delight, already behind us.

In my dreams everything always goes wrong: classrooms of children I can't control, missed buses, lost suitcases. I dream I'm the star of a show called *Celebrity Mousetrap* which is as weird as it sounds. I do not dream of wonderfulness, as others do, like flying over fields of flowers. But in Singapore it smelled of roses and I was finally able to be real with myself again after a long time. The truth, however painful.

ON HOUSE-SITTING

I rest by the koi pond, quietened by the sound of water. The waterlilies open in the morning, close gently each evening, tumble sideways in the small rain. So much beauty in this house, in this garden. Bumpy hard quince, laden damson tree, silver beet, nasturtiums, plums and grapes not yet ready to eat. A shed full of tools and bicycles. A pizza oven waiting, stolid, for another night of dough and olives. Dozens of cookbooks, hundreds of records: music I've always loved, music I've never heard of. One must place the expensive stylus on the vinyl with great concentration. There are two cats, one affectionate, one who might scratch me.

I wash my clothes after weeks of travel. The luxury of a long hot bath. This house is a beautiful place, a creative space. Time to take pause, to sit under the grapes drinking tea from a clay teapot.

I am grieving, having parted from an unsuitable man. So many months of foolishness, of ups and downs and heartache. I wasn't happy with him. I'm not much happier by myself. Not yet. I am confused, sad, angry, alone. I give myself permission to muddle along, lurching from one cup of tea to another.

The cats massacre the silver-foil bag of dry cat food, high on a shelf. One kills a fish from the pond, leaving it wanly dead and gleaming on the lawn. I seal the cat food in a bucket with a lid, put the dead fish in the compost bin, speak to the cats firmly. The murderer, I think, is the one who sleeps on my bed. As for the dead fish, anybody's guess. I'm lucky they didn't eat my face off in the night, dear enormous Cuddles and Rosie.

I walk at evening along the high bank above the sea, sky pale heaven pink and angel blue, making a silent prostration to the sacred island, Rangitoto, trying to love myself, love my life, not indulge in too much gloom. I recall other house-sits: the time I blackened an expensive wooden board and felt the need to repay by leaving my duty-free gin; the time I managed to wreck someone's roller door.

Looking after someone else's house is an in-between thing, an oasis, an occasion of good fortune.

It is time to return to my other life, my Australian life. I clean the fridge, leave cheese, cherries, soup. I burn incense, walking from room to room, scattering blessings. Goodbye, cats. Goodbye, house. Goodbye, New Zealand. If you are born in one country and live in another, you never know which one to call home.

ON THE SPIRITUAL LIFE

The life of one day is enough to rejoice. Even though you live for just one day, if you can be awakened, that one day is vastly superior to one endless life of sleep ... If this day in the lifetime of a hundred years is lost, will you ever touch it with your hands again?

Zen Master Dogen

What does it mean, to live a spiritual life? This is a question that one must answer for oneself. It is a continuing question, a way of being in the world that changes over time and brings its own challenges, demands and delights.

Spirituality is a broad church, but it generally involves a belief in—and a connection to—something beyond a separate small self. It doesn't matter what you choose to call this largeness: God, the Universe, the Sacred, the Tao, the Dharma, a Higher Power, the force of good, The Royal Big or Gloria Zanzibar Magnolia.

I don't see spirituality as a Sunday-in-church affair, or a mystical experience on a silent retreat, although those may be part of it. Our everyday lives are the miracle, and also the living experiment. From the moment you wake until the moment you sleep, every minute is a holy minute. The sacred is to be found in every ordinary thing, when we attend to it with presence and attention. Washing the dog, washing the car, washing the baby, washing the dishes: each one a sacrament.

There are many simple and lovely ways to nourish the spiritual and bring the sacred into daily life:

When you wake in the morning, make a vow to use this day well. It is said that when the dead look down, all they wish for is one more ordinary day. Imagine this is your last day on earth. Give it everything you've got.

Find something bigger than yourself and commit to a deeper relationship with it.

Stay in touch with nature: the tides, the seasons, the birds, the plants. Get your feet on the earth, your toes in the sand. Observe the moon in all her phases. Practise forest bathing and stargazing. Be the earth, laughing in flowers, as Ralph Waldo Emerson suggested in his poem 'Hamatreya'.

Live your own truth. This can mean taking political action, saying no to something or someone, not swallowing popular ideas or believing anything unless you have discovered it to be true for yourself.

Pledge non-violence. Commit to the practice of non-harming. Treat yourself, other people, animals and the planet with reverence. Nourish peace in your heart.

Treat your body kindly. We are all going to die sooner or later but if you look after yourself it is more likely to be later. Feet, eyes, hands, eyebrows, bones, heart, liver, kidney, eyes—all deserving of care and tender attention.

Yoga is not just an exercise. It is a sacred practice involving breath, body and spirit. Anything that brings you into the body can be a spiritual act: tai chi, walking, cycling, dancing.

Play more. Choose a theme for the day and live it: Daring. Joy. Colour. Surprise.

Do something for someone else. Talk to somebody lonely. Make a cake, mind a child, walk a dog, play cards with someone housebound. Loving service is a two-way street, bringing reward to both parties.

Work appreciatively with whatever comes your way. Treat difficulties as opportunities to relax. There is nothing that is not a part of your spiritual life. Dealing with an angry co-worker, remember kindness. Stepping in dog shit, remember laughter. Burning the dinner, remember to pay attention next time. Take every opportunity to be gentle. No blame, no shame, no beating yourself up. Do your best. It will be good enough.

Where we live is our temple. Being creative with colour, fabrics, artwork and found objects is a spiritual occupation. Getting rid of stuff we don't want or need creates space, both literally and metaphorically. The Japanese word *tokonoma* describes a niche or alcove in which something simple and beautiful is displayed, welcoming visitors and uplifting the spirits: a flower, a rock, a scroll. It is refreshed according to the seasons, or on a whim. A shelf or window ledge can serve this purpose.

Take care of things: teeth, gardens, friendships, the planet. Slow down enough to notice what needs doing. In this way we connect with objects, with others, with ourselves. Broken bicycles, messy fridges, cluttered wardrobes, grotty corners: all will benefit from tender care. Children. These we must care for most of all.

Make cooking your spiritual practice, or flower arranging or sewing or drawing. Treat your life as prayer in action. Clean the house as if Jesus was coming to visit.

Slow down. Hurrying, you miss the moment. Hurrying, you miss your life.

Light a candle before dinner. Offer a blessing. There are many wonderful blessings already in existence. Or create your own, or make up a new one every time.

Keep your spiritual energy alive. Take it with you

everywhere. Meet every day and everyone with all the love and acceptance you can muster.

Be an explorer, not a prospector. A prospector is seeking one thing, traditionally gold. The explorer sets out to discover whatever they can find. Let go into the mystery. Gazing at stars may lead you to realise how much you miss your childhood dog. A difficult situation may lead you to strengths you did not know you had. Allow the unknown to be of interest.

When things go badly, cut yourself and everyone else plenty of slack. Make a hot beverage and a delicious little snack, resolving once more to soften and allow. Here you are, in this magnificent life, surrounded by so much beauty, so much strangeness. Where else could you possibly be?

If you are not enjoying your spiritual practice, ask yourself what might enliven it. Do whatever works for you, and when it doesn't, try something else. You are a grown-up now. Teacher Gil Fronsdal threw down an interesting challenge to his students: if the Buddha rocked up and told you that he was sorry but he got it wrong, and none of what he taught was true, what would remain for you? What do you utterly know for yourself, beyond teachers, books and doctrine?

◇◇◇◇◇◇◇◇

As you fall asleep, give thanks for the good things of the day. If nothing comes to mind, give thanks for your bed, the roof over your head, the food in your belly, the water in the tap, your breath. It is simple, noble and brave to be contented with things as they are. To love one's life, without agenda—what could be more holy than this?

Having a spiritual path doesn't have to be that fancy, all that is required is to relax and meet the moment.

This ordinary everyday world, sacred and holy, nothing left out.

ON AN ORDINARY DAY

I wake up in the morning. This in itself is a miracle often taken for granted. I eat avocado on toast for breakfast, drink my tea, have a shower, put on my blue dress and lucky-dice earrings, then walk up the road in the sunshine to post books to my great-nephews. Just an ordinary morning. Just an ordinary day.

I'm off to the climate change rally. It takes me two attempts, because I forget my placard and have to go back for it. There are dozens of teenagers on the platform heading to the city, which is encouraging. On the train I prop *Save the Planet for my Granddaughter* face out against my knee. Opposite me is an older man, handsome, with hippie sandals and a t-shirt adorned with the Aboriginal flag. He puts his hands together and bows in namaste. I feel at one with my tribe and follow the throng to the cathedral, where there is a solid crowd. I run into someone I haven't seen for years, then join my Buddhists For The

Environment friends beside our banner. The sun is strong but we're glad we've showed up. The kids are eloquent, passionate, real, even though the speeches and songs go on a bit too long for me. I've always been impatient and have forgotten to bring my hat. At last we begin to march, along St Georges Terrace, saying what we need to say with our signs and our chants. It's hot and bothery and noisy, but the vibe is relaxed and gentle.

All my life I have marched for freedom, and now I march to save the planet, not just for my granddaughter, but for her granddaughter as well. I wasn't able to find my best friend earlier, due to the big crowd, but now I spot her. She's wearing her battered akubra and looks strong, brown and healthy. We're the same age but I am starting to feel old, cranky and headachey. I should have brought my water.

'This is fun,' she says, a veteran of the successful anti-fracking campaign on the east coast and years of energetic activism. I smile, wanly, because suddenly I am sick of it all, sick of having marched all my life, sick in my guts at how badly the planet is ailing and I hate capitalism and why should these kids have to pay the price of the damage, and what the hell.

We've nearly reached the Convention Centre, where there's apparently a Gas and Mining Industry Convention in progress. I've done my dash. I peel off and stand with my cardboard sign in dappled shade, watching the last of the parade go by. I get talking to the young woman beside me who has stopped to watch. I ask her to take my photo, which she kindly does. Me, under a tree near the corner of William Street and St Georges Terrace, holding my banner, looking sombre.

She tells me she's studying art history at university.

'I'm not sure I'll have children, because of what we have done to the planet,' she confides. She strolls away and I stand there awhile, broken-hearted for her, for all of us.

My headache's getting worse. I give up on my plan to do city errands and head to the station. The lunchtime city workers are busily buying and eating and talking and drinking all manner of fuel-me-up beverages.

I want to shout at them: Stop buying things, you are helping wreck the planet. Also, don't buy fizzy drinks. They are bad for you.

I am turning into a weird old cat lady despite having no cats.

On the train home I'm a messy mixture of hopeful and jaded. I need some lunch and a rest, after my exertion.

My desire for a calm afternoon is not met.

I'm greeted by the news that there has been a terrorist attack in Christchurch. An Australian gunman opens fire in two mosques. Forty-nine people are dead. Many more are injured. I try to comprehend this tragedy, the immense scale and horror of it.

The climate change rally and the shootings, positioned beside each other in some kind of extraordinary counterpoint. I can feel myself going numb. It is not always possible to contain the sorrow of the universe.

Passing my neighbour, a fellow New Zealander, I mention the tragedy in our homeland.

'They're only Muslims, you know,' he says.

I think he must be making some kind of joke. He isn't.

'They think we are infidels. They want to kill us. The mullahs tell them to,' he continues.

I tell him I find his comments distasteful.

'I believe that killing anyone is wrong,' I add.

'You haven't thought it through properly,' he insists.

'We'll have to agree to disagree,' I mumble, grabbing the nearest cliché. 'Let's not make each other miserable about this.'

Inside my door, alone with my shock and horror, my anger and my anguish.

Later in the day I run into him again.

'Are we still speaking to each other?' I ask, with as much equanimity as I can muster. The last thing I want is to be at war with this guy. Up until now he has seemed like a decent person. He cooks for people when they're sick, despite his own poor health.

'I'm glad I saw you. I was worried,' he replies and goes on to explain his views at more length, slightly more moderately. His thinking is deeply embedded, born of fear and racism. His views could not be more opposite to mine. I listen.

'I think the people who died were probably innocent victims,' I offer. He nods. We have a clumsy hug.

Gandhi apparently said that if you can't find God in the next person you meet, it's a waste of time looking for him further. If you subscribe to this idea, then my neighbour and I are God in strange form, stumbling towards Jerusalem in our own clumsy ways.

My little granddaughter asks me what a rally is. I tell her in simple terms.

'Some people are doing harmful things to the planet.'

'I'm not,' she says.

Her small, wise, innocent face is the reason I refuse to surrender to despair and bitterness. I will continue to believe in the decency of most people. I will take to the streets when I have to. I will work towards understanding difference. I will continue to take political action for my own sake, for the sake of my granddaughter, and for the sake of her granddaughter.

◇◇◇◇◇◇◇◇

It is never just an ordinary day. It is a never-before and never-again moment, a day of particles moving through space, arranging and rearranging themselves in ways mysterious, terrifying and miraculous.

FOR TONY HOAGLAND

Goodbye, poet I admired but never met.
I enjoyed your honest, neurotic self,
those bits you offered on the page.
The world you left behind is still plenty weird.
Hugh Hefner's red smoking jacket
fetched $56,847 at auction.
Donald the clown
is not the least bit funny.
Bats are falling dead from the trees.
Soon all the insects will be gone.
In Paris the vegans are attacking the butchers.
It's tempting to be angry about all this but what's the use.
My own confessional: I believe in creativity,
my granddaughter, the ocean, hot beverages.
I'm attached to solitude. Yet lonely.
My dreams are anxious. When I am gone
I'll be remembered for my soups,
for giving each friend the right cartoon.

Halloween. I walk the streets,
enjoying brightly costumed children,
gardens decorated with pumpkins and ghosts.
I am an ancient happy witch.
I have a few verbs, adjectives and nouns to go
before I follow you to the last full stop.

ON THINKING

We live in a world that values thinking more highly than almost anything else. We are schooled to believe that the rational mind is the king, the queen and the ace of diamonds, but thinking can be inaccurate and unreliable. Thoughts are just thoughts. We need them to work out how to get from here to there, how to do our banking and cook palak paneer, but a huge amount of our thinking is unnecessary, obsessive, confusing, conflicted and of limited value. Depression and anxiety have been linked to negative rumination, and the mind becomes agitated when unhelpful thoughts go around and around, leading nowhere in particular or into dark caves of gloom. Buddhist teacher Joseph Goldstein suggests that ninety percent of our thinking could be done without.

Cognitive behavioural therapy (CBT) is a valuable tool, encouraging people to examine their own thinking in order to see if it is conducive to living wisely and cheerfully. Common mistakes are overthinking, catastrophising, black-and-white thinking, and demanding or believing that things should be a certain way rather than accepting life as it is.

The Buddha had not heard the term CBT but he also encouraged people to dwell in wholesome states of mind. He taught that thinking based on kindness, clarity and compassion led to happiness. Being aware of and reframing our thinking takes practice, because often we are truly lost in thought and overwhelmed by an endless loop of judgments, planning, memories, and subtle pathways of petty irritation, impatience, negativity, anxiety and fear. Many of our problems are invented by ourself and our tangled egotistical thinking, which someone witty called Mostly Inaccurate Neurological Drama (MIND).

◇◇◇◇◇◇◇◇

Because we live mainly inside our head, it makes sense to make it a gentle place to be. Our wellbeing is not enhanced when our thinking is motivated by greed, hatred and ignorance. When things seem to be going badly, examining our thoughts to see what effect they are having can bring ease and clarity. Why construct worst-case scenarios for ourself? Why jump to blaming and shaming, or make anything worse by agonising over it and mind-fucking it to death, as Anne Lamott so delicately puts it.

◇◇◇◇◇◇◇◇

It's a powerful, liberating act to take control of our thinking and point it towards good cheer. My friend Bridget Kalo taught me a great way of responding when she received a bill. Instead of thinking how awful it was and how short of money she was, she told herself *I'm glad I have the money to pay this.* She then paid it willingly and forgot about it.

When feeling overwhelmed, close to the edge, ragged, fragile or panicky, what is the most gentle thing to tell yourself? It probably isn't *I can't cope. Everybody hates me. Life is shit and nothing will ever be any good again.* Better to reassure yourself that although the moment is tricky, all that's actually happening is bodily sensations and thoughts, and that they are temporary.

Take some good deep breaths and relax into the body, allowing the sensations. Then provide more supportive thinking. *This too will pass. These are just feelings. It's okay. This will sort out.* If it helps, lie down, go for a walk, or sit quietly in the sun until a sense of calm returns.

In my own case, I've found this technique useful with my insomnia. Usually I have no problem falling asleep but occasionally, when overtired and overstimulated, I descend into a dark, scary mind space, becoming more and more anxious, unable to relax and drift off. Sometimes I get up, as advised by sleep experts, who suggest rising, doing something relaxing, then going back to bed when one feels sleepy. The trouble is, at three am, exhausted, this is the last thing I want to do. I sometimes take a sliver of valium, but it leaves me groggy the next day and knocking myself out is not a real solution to an ongoing problem.

Instead, I've begun doing a body scan, softening and allowing. I quieten the voice saying I'm going downhill and will end up in a locked psych ward, thin as a twig and completely mad. As you can imagine, this line of thought is neither helpful nor pleasant. Also, it is not true. I remind myself that thoughts are just thoughts, and that these ones are unwise, corrosive and not to my advantage. Instead I say something much nicer to myself.

Don't worry, honey. This happens sometimes. It happens to everybody. Tomorrow will be okay, even if you are a bit tired. Would you like to get up and drink a chamomile tea and draw a nice flower? Or would you just like to snuggle down and drift off? It's okay, sweetie. No need to fret.

This usually does the trick. If not, I play a game I've invented in which I list the things I am lucky to have. Tea towels. A ripe avocado. Slippers. Elbows. A picture of Lakshmi, the Hindu goddess of wealth and prosperity, wearing a precious jewel in her belly. Coloured pencils. Toilet paper. Pretty scarves. A letterbox.

Ad infinitum until voila, I wake up and it's morning.

Our thinking creates our universe. When we take responsibility for it, training our minds towards the light, we are no longer making a problem of ourself—or for ourself.

Your equanimity and contentment depend on the quality of your thinking. No medicine, no shrink, or any guru can do this work for you, but don't worry, you only have to do it from now until always. Sometimes you don't have to do a thing. The day flows gently, and your thoughts are wholesome and wise. But when mental agitation, negativity, worry, gloom and despair assail you, soften your belly and manifest a plenitude of kind thinking. Seeing your mind is all stories, you might as well tell yourself good ones.

BORDER LINES

Avalokiteshvara's kid won't get off the computer,
Shakyamuni waits in line at Centrelink,
Dogen's therapist is trying him on Prozac,
Lin Chi left her husband for another man.

Five transcendental Buddhas are going through the menopause,
Bodhidharma's daughter wears sexy lipstick and ten-hole Docs,
Wu-men's ex gave me a crystal and some rose geranium oil,
Green Tara's mother is learning to play bridge.

Ganesha waves her many arms, holding out a lifestyle magazine,
a slice of designer pizza and a glass of chardonnay.
Joshu got burgled. They stole his Mastercard.

Vimalakirti chose Optus.
Dorje Chang dyed her hair a splendid ruby red.

I saw Kanzeon, goddess of compassion,
in a car park. She just smiled and winked at me.

LIFE LESSONS

I can see some of you sticking your fingers down your throat and making fake gagging noises when you read this title.

'Too Oprah, too hippie, too New Age, too preachy, too something,' you mutter.

But really, what have we learned, here in life school?

I have learned, sometimes the hard way, that keeping on doing anything that brings a poor result counts as headbanging and I might as well stop doing it. In this category I would put complaining, expecting other people to change to meet my expectations, overdoing anything, people-pleasing, worrying, freaking out about everything, judging other people, and buying tight shoes or clothes that are cheap and almost okay.

That you can't do anything about the past except take a good clear look at it, frame it in the most positive light, and move on. For example, in my case, yes, my parents were hard yards, but they brought me into this world, and fed and clothed me. They taught me how to make a decent omelette, how to live well on bugger-all, how to throw a good party. They instilled in me a respect for education and a love of books, art, poetry and music. From their mistakes I learned that free love isn't really free, and from their early tragic deaths I have learned how to be resilient and that family is really important. Thank you, Bob and Irene.

I have learned from fine spiritual teachers that you can't do shit about most of what happens, but if you take responsibility for your actions, act kindly, cultivate contentment and act with good cheer, the present moment feels a whole lot better.

I have learned not to seek eternal happiness in possessions, career, fame, relationships or endless exotic holidays. Better to appreciate what I have and enjoy it fully, no longer subscribing to Paradise Is Somewhere Else.

I have learned that some relationships just don't work and if I am not flourishing within them I must let go of them, and this is hard.

I have learned that it is good to stand up for what I believe in, knowing the world will always be a major disaster in ways that I can't change.

I have learned to appreciate everything. Especially bees. One day they will be gone and so will I. For now, I am in Earth School and I have much to learn.

ON GRATITUDE AND JOY

The amygdala, part of the limbic system in the brain, looks out for disaster, wiring us to expect the worst. A tiger might be coming at you, any second now! This was once useful information if a tiger *was* actually coming at you, but unfortunately it can now mean we live anxiously and fearfully, anticipating dangers that do not exist.

Positive mind states, such as joy and gratitude, can be cultivated. This is good to do, especially if low mood is your default position.

Nourishing positive mind states can be a practice at any time, in any moment. There is always something to appreciate: a flower, a smile, the aroma of your coffee. 'There is only one heroism in the world: to see the world as it is, and love it', as the novelist and idealist Romain Rolland wisely points out.

These are some of the things I am grateful for:

my son
his wife
my granddaughters
my entire family, actually
vegetables
rice
walking
swimming
reading
live music
chai with honey
sunsets
stars
Indian ragas
hugs
sleep
movies
my friends
therapy
journalling
soft rugs
colourful clothing
gardens
long walks

living in a country that is not war-torn
jazz
motown
rivers
curry
potatoes
mangoes
sparkly jewels
kimonos
giraffes
bicycles
yoga
my fave café
libraries
books beside my bed
fabrics, threads, beads, paper, paint

Do not underestimate the power of using a gratitude journal. Even at the end of the toughest day, you'll be surprised how much goodness you can find. If you don't connect with the idea of gratitude, find a word that resonates for you, such as contentment, joy or ease. List your blessings, bowing to the generosity of this precious life.

ON QUESTIONS

What conditions do you need to thrive?
Where have you been lately? Where are you headed?
What interests you? What do you fancy? What did you love as a child?
What in your life is not supporting your spiritual growth?
Are you currently your own best friend or your own worst enemy?
What do you do for you? What do you do for others? Are these two lists in balance?
How can you nourish yourself in ways that don't cost any money?
What self-care have you done today? What self-care could you do tomorrow?
Can you be contented with the way things are, without anyone else changing their behaviour to accommodate you?

If you are facing a challenge, what would Buddha, Jesus, or the wisest person you know do in this situation?
How would it be to give up your most painful thought?
How would you live if you only had a year to live? Since you don't know how long you've got, why not live this way anyway?
What is your most important thing?
Make a list of ten wonders, three adventures and one promise to yourself.

ON DECISION-MAKING

Most people find decision-making tricky. Some of us find it extremely tricky. I've been known to have an existential crisis about the simplest of decisions, let alone more complex ones. I don't always have a clear compass as to what I feel and need, with ensuing speed wobbles regarding making clear choices. I'm not alone in this. As one person commented in a group for Adult Children of Alcoholics, 'I know there's such a thing as steady. I see it as I swing by.'

Here are some strategies I've learned which help with decision-making.

If we believe there is a right and a wrong decision, and we don't know which is which, it can be crippling. If we assume that any choice is viable, it makes the whole matter easier. Nothing will be perfect, so we might as well relax. The Persian poet Rumi said 'Live life as if everything is rigged in your favour'. How beautiful things become when we trust the world and anticipate good results instead of disaster.

If you seek a wise and gentle solution, use your wisest and most gentle energy. Are you operating from love or from fear? Solutions born of negativity will rarely be the best ones so tune into your creative playful energy rather than broadcasts from the Land of Dread.

Sometimes it is good to just not decide. No need to wrestle the problem to the ground. Just let it go and see what evolves, because the world will come up with a solution, given time. It takes patience to leave things alone, but if things are murky we probably don't have full information yet. Taking one's hands off the steering wheel can be an intelligent strategy, at least metaphorically. As my Zen teacher says, when things feel urgent, Immediately Do Nothing. Taoist philosophy believes you can achieve great things by going with the flow. This requires trust in the flow. Again, if you believe that the world is rigged in your favour, perhaps you will be delighted by what comes your way.

When you are stressed, lying down is good. So is a meditative cup of tea. A long walk is excellent. Don't waste too much time on small unimportant decisions. With the ones that really matter, enjoy the luxury of spaciousness. Let yourself swing back and forth until clarity manifests.

Resist the urge to swing things prematurely to Yes or No, in order to avoid the vulnerability of ambiguity. It's fine to Not Know. Becoming comfortable with uncertainty brings ease.

Too many choices make things complicated. Option overload leads to bewilderment so, when possible, narrow your options down to two. Trust your intuition. Often there is clarity in listening to your gut, your heart, your common sense. If an intuitive answer is not apparent, employ your rational mind. Ask a couple of questions which have a yes/no answer such as: Does this align with my deepest values? Is it comfortable and safe? Sometimes just going with what is simplest and easiest is a good idea.

Once a decision is made, commit. Keep going forwards and don't look back, unless you've been pressed into something unduly, in which case, change your mind. Say you've had time to think and it's not going to work for you. Remember the Turkish proverb: *No matter how far you have gone on the wrong track, turn back.*

On the other hand, be aware of constant mind-changing. Agitation and confusion lead to more agitation and confusion. Buyer's remorse is a classic scenario. It's common to have a tumble of anxiety and regret immediately after making a large purchase. This is part of being human. Your mind is a whirlwind, but it is also a place of ease, at least some of the time. Remember that nothing will be perfect, whatever you do. Aim for good enough. Treat yourself like a dear little fractious child who needs snacks and treats, and look out the window for a while, because the birds and clouds and sky and leaves are still there and the day is worth savouring, and most of your troubles are ones you make up for yourself.

ON THE SINGING HEART KITCHEN

I cook because I am hungry. I cook because I need to eat. I cook because the Hindu guru and mystic Neem Karoli Baba said *love people and feed them*, and I believe him to be right.

I cook because it earths me, because sometimes it is the only thing that makes sense. I cook because if I stew flavourless plums and top them with almonds, oats, butter, sugar and cinnamon, they will taste excellent.

I cook because fetta is perfect with spinach, and cauliflower is wonderful roasted, and so are tomatoes and potatoes and in fact any vegetable. Except perhaps the pea. Yes, not the pea.

Dogen said you should never waste a grain of rice. In his honour I became the Queen of Everything Soup. It is my superpower and involves staring into the refrigerator and thinking, in order to keep ahead of ancient produce. Nothing gets wasted in my house. Everything is eaten, frozen, blended, shared or baked in a big casserole and eaten with crusty bread. Creativity is the art of making something out of nothing, a new thing out of other things. Old bread transforms into breadcrumbs, or crunchy croutons or a strata—a tasty baked dish of bread, eggs, herbs, cheese and cream. If you can't work out what to do with an aging vegetable, cook it, season it, blend it, add a slosh of cream and call it soup.

Fun Facts about Food: You can tell a lot about someone by the way they cook, and the way they eat. Mangoes are hard to get out from between your teeth but they are worth it. There is no middle way with the love-me or hate-me flavours of coriander and licorice.

Things to Remember in a Kitchen: Wash your hands before preparing food. Use all the colours, all the food groups. Cook seasonally: asparagus in springtime, pears in autumn, berries and stone fruit in summer, root vegetables and long slow stews in winter. Relax and enjoy it. Wear a retro apron, listen to your fave music while drying the dishes. Cook fully and completely. Cook with love. Cook with gratitude, eat with devotion. You are one of the lucky ones.

Secret Confession: Once upon a time, in the late afternoon, I threw away some yoghurt that had gone beyond. Even Google had no uses for going-bad-yoghurt.

I decided not to poison my friends or make my soup taste weird and threw it in the compost. All hail the compost bin.

ON TRAVEL

I've been thinking about travelling or rather I've been thinking about not travelling. This began as a way of lessening my ecological footprint, but it has become a deeper contemplation since at present travel is impossible, due to the pandemic.

For most of my life, the here and now has seemed unpalatable. Somewhere else has always held greater promise. My restless mind and productive imagination love to create something better, later. I think it fair to say that I am not alone in this delusion, which Zen teacher Robert Aitken once described as 'seeking better accommodation elsewhere.'

An example. While eating my breakfast today, a wave of messy sorrow threatened to dump me. Who knows what caused its arrival? Perhaps it was triggered by the uncertainty of the days to come, or yesterday's difficult phonecall. The heart and mind have their own mysterious rhythms and reasons but there it was, a deep soup of sadness. On with the day, I told myself.

However, as I muddled onwards, a raft of escape ideas came my way, none of them currently viable.

It's an old game, imagining that by doing a geographical you can outrun yourself.

The trouble is, as Jon Kabat Zinn puts it, wherever we go, there we are. If we have anger, it will manifest in an airline queue. If we are anxious, we'll be anxious in Bangkok or Berlin. Probably more so, given the crazy traffic in Bangkok. If the mind is dissatisfied, we'll manage to find fault, even in the most elegant location.

Now that it is futile to idly check the airline fares and I must cease my pleasant imaginings about a holiday in Bali, I get a chance to have a clear look at my discontent. What is it that stops me loving my life, exactly as it is? Why am I not satisfied with my apartment, my clothes, this evening's pale sunset? Why do I hurry to the next bit, ignoring the feel of my feet on the grass, the scent of roses? I miss so much living this way. Can I not sit quietly on my balcony, watching the birds, drinking tea slowly, not wanting to be anywhere else.

I'm reminded of a Victoria Roberts cartoon in which the woman gaily tells her stolid armchair-bound husband that she is going to France, because she is a different person there. Maybe, I reflect, if Bali brings out the colourful hippie in me, I could access her more fully here in my life, no airfare required.

Many travels don't go according to plan. Our plans do not include airplane delays, lost luggage, jet lag, rude people, boredom or terrorist attacks. Nor do they include pandemics. *Escape*, the travel poster invites, but there is no escape from the transitoriness of phenomena or the aches of the human heart. In the end, there is nowhere to go but here, no-one special to be, and no joy like the taste of the present moment.

Perhaps to stay present to what is current, what is real, is the biggest adventure. Travel can bring a thousand blessings, but it can also be a mere strategy for accumulating photographs, as Susan Sontag noted. Sometimes the planning and the remembering is tastier than the doing. Wholesale tourism has wrought many negative consequences to places such as Bali, and I am cheered and humbled to learn that without international tourism there has been a renewal of cottage industry, such as tempe production. Young people from the restaurant and hotel trades have returned to their villages, bringing new energy, and this can only be a good thing.

This is not to say that one should not travel. Experiencing other cultures can bring joy, insight, learning and connection, but in this changing world perhaps we can learn to enjoy smaller adventures, closer to home.

Last thoughts. Clean everything in sight before you go travelling so that if you die when you are away, people will not only miss you, they will remember you as being exceptionally tidy. Furthermore, when you travel, you will always bring the wrong clothes, and forget at least two things. It will not matter.

FOLLOWING THE MOON HOME

for Aitken Roshi

It slides like a blob of butter
low down in the sky,
almost not moon
tricking us into believing
it is something else,
although we can't think what.
Disguised as a fat, flying shape
hiding behind tall buildings,
finally appearing again as moon.

Tonight we listened to the Zen master,
haiku scholar, old smile, wise man.
His words give power to the night.

We talk and are happy.
Just this,
following the moon home.

ON SITTING QUIETLY

Spoiler alert. There is suffering. The Buddha described our predicament like this:

> *The suffering of birth.*
> *The suffering of old age.*
> *The suffering of illness.*
> *The suffering of death.*
> *The suffering of encountering what is unpleasant.*
> *The suffering of separation from what is pleasant.*
> *The suffering of not getting what one wants.*

We do not like the truth of this predicament. We secretly hope that if we eat properly, exercise diligently and play nice we'll cunningly avoid that awful stuff; if we just make the right moves we'll stay out of trouble.

It doesn't work. People we love will die. Our bodies will behave badly. Children get cancer. Human beings kill other human beings. Ecologically we are looking pretty screwed. However many petitions we sign or acts of kindness we perform, the fire of human suffering cannot be quelled.

Knowing that all meetings will end in partings and that death is our final destination can make life seem futile and unsatisfying. This doesn't mean that joy and merriment do not come our way, but being human is inherently fragile, however furiously we rearrange the deckchairs on the *Destiny Ace.*

So, why meditate? Why not just continue seeking happiness in the temporal? Turn away from the spiritual, get as much pleasure for yourself as you can, and keep on trucking? That is indeed one option. It's the path many travel.

Others choose a different road. As one Tibetan sage put it, we sit 'to make a difficult situation better'.

Life contains hardship, but there is something straightforward about coming to terms with reality. By regularly disengaging from the ceaseless demands of the world, we create breathing room. Counterintuitively, by staying still with our feelings, the sensations in our body and the silence beneath them, we become more able to enjoy the world, no long so overwhelmed by the uncertainty of the human condition. When we slow down, we taste our lives fully—the flavour of happiness, the flavour of grief.

We discover reserves of strength, ease, equanimity and patience we did not know we had, which serve us well when strong winds blow.

If we do not have the wisdom to foster awareness, our lives can become a tangle of addictive behaviours and avoidant strategies. Excessive alcohol and recreational drugs are what Buddhist teacher Josh Korda calls failed attempts at happiness, providing a temporary release from difficult feelings but leading to a whole host of other troubles. Compulsive shopping, screen bingeing, staying very busy, and endlessly trying to control other people are similarly doomed attempts.

It is not only for ourselves that we sit. When we attend to our own life with delicacy and care, there is positive benefit for those around us and the wider community. If we stay present in difficult conditions, if we can listen deeply and do our quiet best in every situation, we will indeed 'shine one corner', as Suzuki Roshi said.

Meditation does not need to be a scary, difficult or ambitious project. Start with five minutes. Take a relaxed upright posture and sit. Focus on the breath, bodily sensations, or your entire experience: thinking, breathing, sounds, longing, restless mind, sleepy mind, whatever naturally arises. There's nothing more fancy or more complicated about it than that.

Just sitting means just that. No need to transform or improve your experience. Let everything be as it is, relaxing into a gentle, allowing presence.

Sitting brings us into our lives, plain and simple, so that we know things as they are, taste their flavour, calmly abiding with changing conditions. Sitting helps us live fully and respond fully, in the most appropriate way, not endlessly seeking pleasure, nor hiding from suffering.

Take pleasure in the breath. Let whatever arises be all right by you. Everything else will take care of itself.

THINGS NOT WRITTEN ABOUT

A leaf falling through loneliness. A cloud calling your name. The beautiful inconvenient rain. The overanxious guest, the almost-Christmas morning. The allure of bourgeois success. The complicated silence, the unwise impulse, the forgotten thought. The languid pulse of time. The unintelligible language of birds. My various dressing-gowns. Ancient charms. Heart flower. Rain flower. Stolen flowers. Ancient mistakes. The virtues of tofu. The downfall of the Third Reich. The next bit.

NOTES AND ACKNOWLEDGEMENTS

Thanks to my teachers and friends over time whose names appear in this book. Sources have been attributed and permission sought for usage wherever possible.

p. 9 Anne Lamott, '12 Truths I Learned from Life and Writing', dailygood.org/story/2187/12-truths-i-learned-from-life-and-writing.

p. 24 Jeff Foster, 'Why Life Is Never As Bad As You Think', lifewithoutacentre.com/writings/why-life-is-never-as-bad-as-you-think.

p. 32 The Krishnamurti story appears in Jim Dreaver, *End Your Story, Begin Your Life: Wake Up, Let Go, Live Free*, Hampton Roads, 2012.

p. 33 Suzuki Roshi in Edward Espe Brown, 'When You Are You, Zen Is Zen' in *Will Yoga & Meditation Really Change My Life?*, Stephen Cope (ed.), Storey Publishing, 2012, p. 125.

p. 38 Ezra Bayda with Elizabeth Hamilton, *Aging For Beginners*, Wisdom Publications, 2018.

p. 47 Johann Hari, *Lost Connections: Uncovering the Real Causes of Depression—and the Unexpected Solutions*, Bloomsbury, 2019.

p. 49 Jean-Paul Sartre, *No Exit* (*Huis Clos*), Pearson, 1962 (first published 1944).

p. 52 Joseph Goldstein, 'Mindfulness—The Real Deal, Beyond the Buzz', *Rewire Me,* rewireme.com/wellness/mindfulness-a-practical-guide-to-awakening-by-joseph-goldstein.

p. 64 Julia Cameron, 'Morning Pages', newyorkwritersintensive.com/wp-content/uploads/2012/05/morningpages.pdf.

p. 64 Natalie Goldberg, *Writing Down the Bones: Freeing the Writer Within,* Shambhala, 2016, p. 172.

p. 69 John Patrick (screenplay), *Love Is a Many-Splendored Thing,* 1955.

p. 84 Jack Kerouac, *On the Road,* Penguin, 2000 (first published 1957).

p. 86 Nguyen Anh-Huong and Thich Nhat Hanh, *Walking Meditation: Easy Steps to Mindfulness,* Boulder: Sounds True, 2006. See also Thich Nhat Hanh, *Peace Is Every Step: The Path of Mindfulness in Everyday Life*, Colorado: Bantam Books, 1992.

p. 95 Ralph Waldo Emerson, 'Hamatreya', *Poets of the English Language,* W.H. Auden and Norman Holmes Pearson (eds), Viking Press, 1950; available online from poetryfoundation.org/poems/52341/hamatreya.

p. 98 To access the talks of Gil Fronsdal visit audiodharma.org/teacher/1.

p. 110 Anne Lamott, *Operating Instructions: A Journal of My Son's First Year,* Anchor Books, 2005, p. 112.

p. 117 Romain Rolland, *The Life of Michael Angelo,* Frederic Lees (trans.), E.P. Dutton and Company, 1912.

p. 126 Neem Karoli Baba in Ram Dass, 'Love Everyone: Lessons in Compassion', yogainternational.com/article/view/love-everyone-lessons-in-compassion.

p. 130 Jon Kabat-Zinn, *Wherever You Go There You Are: Mindfulness Meditation in Everyday Life*, Hachette, 2005.

p. 130 Victoria Roberts, 'Let's go to France' cartoon, fineartamerica.com/featured/im-going-to-france-im-a-different-person-victoria-roberts.html.

p. 136 Salvador Pantoja interview with Josh Korda, 'How a "Dharma Punk" Learned to Treat Addiction through Meditation', in asiasociety.org/new-york/how-dharma-punk-learned-treat-addiction-through-meditation.

p. 136 David Chadwick, *To Shine One Corner of the World: Moments with Shunryu Suzuki*, Broadway, 2001.

Brigid Lowry began her writing career by self-publishing two dreadful poems when she was eight. She spent her twenties living in a Buddhist community, veered into performance poetry in her thirties, and subsequently survived two marriages, raised a fine son and wrote eight award-winning young adult books. Her first essay collection, *Still Life with Teapot: On Zen, Memoir and Creativity*, was published in 2016. She is a poet, a Zen student, a creative writing teacher, an introvert who talks too fast, a drifter and dreamer who loves the world of words. Brigid believes in nectarines, coloured pencils and op shops, and in living with authenticity and joy.

First published 2021 by
FREMANTLE PRESS

Fremantle Press Inc. trading as Fremantle Press
25 Quarry Street, Fremantle WA 6160
(PO Box 158, North Fremantle WA 6159)
www.fremantlepress.com.au

Cover image: Ruth de Vos, *Maddi's Flowers*, ruthdevos.com.
Design: Carolyn Brown, tendeersigh.com.au.
Printed by Everbest Printing Investment Limited, China.

A catalogue record for this book is available from the National Library of Australia

ISBN 9781925816327 (paperback)
ISBN 9781925816334 (ebook)

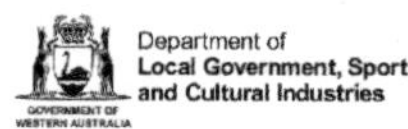

Fremantle Press is supported by the State Government through the Department of Local Government, Sport and Cultural Industries.

Publication of this title was assisted by the Commonwealth Government through the Australia Council, its arts funding and advisory body.